Unmasking
Apocalyptic Texts

Unmasking Apocalyptic Texts

A GUIDE TO PREACHING AND TEACHING

Dorothy Jonaitis

Tessie,

Blessings in hope as you walk toward God.

Dorothy, OP

Paulist Press
New York/Mahwah, N.J.

Cover design by Sharyn Banks
Book design by Lynn Else

Library of Congress Cataloging-in-Publication Data

Jonaitis, Dorothy.
    Unmasking apocalyptic texts : a guide to preaching and teaching / Dorothy Jonaitis.
       p. cm.
    Includes bibliographical references.
    ISBN 0-8091-4356-9 (alk. paper)
    1. Apocalyptic literature. I. Title.
    BS646.J65 2005
    220'.046—dc22

                                      2005012205

Published by Paulist Press
997 Macarthur Boulevard
Mahwah, New Jersey 07430

www.paulistpress.com

Printed and bound in the
United States of America

To
My sister Kathi,
and to
Frannie, Eleanor, and Mary
Diane, Lucille, and Linn
Together We Walked
with Hands and Hearts as One
toward Easter Hope

LET US NOT BE DISHEARTENED,
    even when the horizon of history grows dim and closes in,
as though human realities made impossible
the accomplishment of God's plans.
God makes use even of human errors,
    even of human sins,
    so as to make rise over the darkness what Isaiah spoke of.
One day prophets will sing
    not only the return from Babylon
    but our full liberation.
"The people that walked in darkness have seen a great light.
They walk in lands of shadows,
    but a light has shone forth."

—*Oscar Romero*[1]

CONTENTS

ILLUSTRATIONS

TABLES

FIGURES

PREFACE

Many imaginative people inspired this book. The Grand Rapids Dominicans committed to women studying theology and preaching for the benefit of the Dominican Order and the church, trusted my ability, and provided financial support. I am grateful to the leadership team, but especially to Barbara Hansen, OP, for her generous and caring support.

The faculty of Aquinas Institute of Theology is acknowledged for their dedication to the formation of women preachers. Individual mention is given to Gregory Heille, OP, and George Boudreau, OP, but especially to Joan Delaphane, OP, for her care and concern as my thesis director. Bernhard Asen, PhD, from St. Louis University was instrumental in assisting me with the apocalyptic chapters. Special thanks to Jana Childers, PhD, Homiletics Professor at San Francisco Theological School, whose gifts of imagination and drama encouraged me. Gratitude is also expressed to Sally Gunter and Ron Crown for valuable library advice.

Particular thanks to Andrew Carl Wisdom, OP, for friendship, support, and challenge. He is truly my brother in both the Christian and Dominican sense. He helped me with proofreading chapters and checking footnotes and overall encouragement as I completed my thesis. Since this book began with my Doctor of Ministry thesis project, I am most grateful to Steve Mueller, who shepherded me through that project. His gift for seeing the fine points is evident in this work.

A special thanks is given to Fr. Lawrence Boadt, General Editor at Paulist Press, for believing in my work and deciding to submit it for publication. Thanks also to Paul McMahon and to Nancy de Flon, my editor at Paulist Press, whose critical eyes have helped me with polishing the fine points of this work. Nancy was always welcoming of my ideas, thoughts, and suggestions.

Extraordinary thanks to family and friends on life's journey, in particular those named in the dedication. They provided supportive prayer and continued encouragement in this work and in other life issues that keep the hope-filled journey interesting.

I know this work could not have been done without the grace of God, who has guided my journey through all its ups and downs and still kept me hopeful. May God be praised through the endeavors that keep my life exciting and to all future tasks yet to be accomplished in the glory of God.

ACKNOWLEDGMENTS

Some material in this book was originally published in the following journals and is used with permission of the author: Dorothy Jonaitis, OP, "The Victory of the Lamb," *The Bible Today* (November 1993): 366–70. Dorothy Jonaitis, OP, "Dramatic Reading of Apocalyptic Literature Leads to Hope," in Alan Lenzi, ed., *Proceedings of the Central States Regional Meeting of the Society of Biblical Literature and the American Schools of Oriental Research*, Vol. 5 (Spring 2002): 47–71.

Excerpt from Introduction to *New Poems* [from *Collected Poems*]. Copyright 1938, © 1966, 1991 by the Trustees for the E. E. Cummings Trust, from *Complete Poems: 1904–1962* by E. E. Cummings, edited by George Firmage. Used by permission of Liveright Publishing Corporation.

Excerpts from *Letters to a Young Poet* by Rainer Maria Rilke. Copyright © 2000. Used with permission from New World Library, Novato, CA 94949.

From *Isaiah: Spirit of Courage, Gift of Tears* by Daniel Berrigan. Copyright © 1996 Augsburg Fortress. Used by permission.

From *The Survivor and Other Poems* by Tadeusz Rozewicz. Copyright © 1976 by Princeton University Press. Reprinted by permission of Princeton University Press.

Final four lines from "Dedication" from *The Collected Poems 1931–1987* by Czeslaw Milosz. Copyright © 1988 by Czeslaw Milosz Royalties, Inc. Reprinted by permission of HarperCollins Publishers Inc.

Excerpt from Amos Wilder, "Electric Chimes and Ram's Horns," *Reader's Digest*, July 1960, p. 2; quoted in *Christian Century 88* (27 January 1971): 105.

The diagram on p. 150 is reproduced from Fritz West, *Scripture and Memory: The Ecumenical Hermeneutic of the Three-Year Lectionaries*, published by The Liturgical Press, 1997. Used with permission. All rights reserved.

ABBREVIATIONS

FIRST TESTAMENT

Gen	Genesis	Prov	Proverbs
Exod	Exodus	Isa	Isaiah
Josh	Joshua	Jer	Jeremiah
Judg	Judges	Ezek	Ezekiel
2 Sam	2 Samuel	Dan	Daniel
1 Kgs	1 Kings	Mic	Micah
2 Chr	2 Chronicles	Hab	Habakkuk
Ezra	Ezra	Hag	Haggai
Neh	Nehemiah	Zech	Zechariah
Ps	Psalms	1 Macc	1 Maccabees
Joel	Joel	2 Macc	2 Maccabees
Amos	Amos		
Jonah	Jonah		

SECOND TESTAMENT

Matt	Matthew	1 John	1 John
Mark	Mark	Gal	Galatians
Luke	Luke	Eph	Ephesians
John	John	Phil	Philippians
Acts	Acts of the Apostles	1 Thess	1 Thessalonians
Rom	Romans	2 Thess	2 Thessalonians
1 Cor	1 Corinthians	Heb	Hebrews
2 Cor	2 Corinthians	Rev	Revelation
1 Pet	1 Peter		

DATES

BCE   Before the Common Era   CE   Common Era

BIBLE TRANSLATIONS

NABR   Revised New American Bible
NIV   New International Version
NIV Interlinear   New International Version of English text with Greek complement
NJB   New Jerusalem Bible
NRSV   New Revised Standard Version
REB   Revised English Bible
TNK   Tanakh, the English Version of the Jewish Bible

GLOSSARY OF TERMS

Apocalypse A literary genre with a narrative framework intended for a group in crisis, addressing renewal of faith and reordering of life because of a vision experienced by a human recipient but mediated by an otherworldly being who tends to relativize existing realities superseded by God's universal reign. Temporal as well as spatial, it visualizes eschatological salvation in a supernatural world. The eschatological event will unfold, true to an eternal plan, as a result of divine action.

Apocalypticism A social worldview influenced by beliefs associated with apocalyptic literature.

Armageddon That place connected with Mount Megiddo where the last battle between good and evil is said to take place and God's final reign of glory would be in its fullness.

Babylon City on the left bank of the Euphrates River not far from modern-day Baghdad; in biblical history, the place of exile of the Jewish elite when Jerusalem was destroyed by the Babylonians (587 BCE). Babylon is often a metaphor for the city of wickedness, where all evil dwells.

Day of the Lord The final day of judgment for the whole world, when God will triumph over evil and reign forever.

Eschatology A theological term describing the end times or the last things (Greek, eschaton), that is, heaven, hell, death, and judgment.

Pseudonymous A term ascribing authorship falsely to a venerable figure of past history instead of naming the real author. Apocalyptic literature is most often pseudonymous, and the real authors are seldom known.

Qumran A complex of buildings near the Dead Sea in which a community of Jewish sectarians lived. From the scrolls found in the area in 1947 (called the Dead Sea Scrolls), scholars learned that the group believed that the Teacher of Righteousness, their leader, would help them be pure and holy for God.

Septuagint (LXX, Greek for seventy) The Greek translation of the Hebrew Bible written in Egypt beginning about 250 BCE. It also included several books written in Greek. Early Greek-speaking Christians adopted this Bible. The LXX abbreviation, commonly used for this translation, comes from a legend according to which seventy scholars translated the Hebrew at different times and places and all resulted in exactly the same text.

Do not be misled by the great number
of names and the complexity of cases.
Perhaps there is overall a great
Motherhood expressed as mutual longing.
—*Rainer Maria Rilke* [1]

Introduction

ON THE PATH TOWARD THE ETERNAL PRESENCE

The journey toward God is intrinsically charged with hope-filled action. But action alone is dead without divine guidance. People must be able to imagine God who deeply sensitizes them, whose mysterious footprints walk in the tenuous sand of their world. One tool for imagining God's divine providence is contained in the apocalyptic texts of the Bible, if they are understood properly. A recent article in *Time* magazine (July 1, 2002) indicates that many people take these texts literally and not with imagination.

Perhaps the lack of imagination comes from the literature itself. It can be so stark that it only elicits *hell and damnation* fears from which many desperately flee. When, if ever, have people heard a hope-filled sermon (homily[2]) on apocalyptic literature? Hope can be generated when we understand the rationale for apocalyptic texts and preach the essence of the divine message they embody.

Since September 11, 2001, the question of hope, more than faith, has arisen for many. People have felt extremely insecure. Their once protected lives seem now utterly vulnerable, which makes them turn to God for answers to their confusion.

Living in the midst of crisis, people tend to view salvation as a journey of decisions between good and evil, where decisions toward good cannot occur without being anchored in a hope-

filled God. Hope in the midst of crisis—that journey will be introduced to teachers, preachers, and imaginative readers. In fact, that
journey faced by all humans makes this a book not only for us, but
also for all who imagine with hope while attending to crisis. It is
a journey toward the Eternal Presence, who will sustain humanity
in hope beyond any disaster.

Jana Childers speaks of the cosmic struggle as one between life
and death and suggests that it forms the backbone of every
Christian sermon. But, she also recognizes that the individual
struggle with good and evil fleshes out each new moment and
helps us imagine God's grace. That cosmic struggle, accompanied
by the daily, personal struggles of those who face the magnitude
of evil in our twenty-first century, is at the heart of preaching,
teaching, and imagining from apocalyptic texts.[3]

While preparing an apocalyptic sermon or teaching, we
embrace both struggles. We feel the daily personal struggles while
we, like the apocalyptic writer, make an effort to preach and teach
dramatically and forcefully that *God ultimately wins over all evil.* In
times of greatest need or difficulty, we are called to be as confident
as the apocalyptic writer, who articulated hopefully that God was
victorious over every evil of their time.

Are we confident and hopeful? Or are we woefully inadequate
to the task? Answers to these questions depend upon our understanding of the function of apocalyptic texts. But when have we
learned this? David Buttrick expressed concern that no study
exists on how to preach apocalyptic texts. He laments that fact
because of the apocalyptic "strands of thought" in our own age.[4]
It seems that Buttrick is seriously questioning whether one can be
taught to preach and teach from apocalyptic texts as well. This
book guides readers into hopeful preaching, teaching, and imagining of apocalyptic literature, contributing to the void noted by
Buttrick. Besides giving solid, concrete suggestions for teaching
and preaching, it also provides a crisis model for understanding
these texts in a more general way.

An article published as the world turned the corner to a new
millennium strongly confirms the need for imaginative, hope-
filled apocalyptic preaching and teaching. Reflecting upon
Jonathan Schell's book, *The Fate of the Earth*, George W. E.

Nickelsburg objected to Schell's thesis "that a nuclear war could bring an end to human history and human life on earth."[5] Nickelsburg noted that Schell's concept of the world's end is dramatically different from the apocalyptic biblical picture of that end. First, Schell's scenario of humanity demolishing evil by way of nuclear devastation indicates that humans are more powerful than God, thus negating God. Second, Nickelsburg objects to Schell's negativity toward the hopes attached to biblical accounts of judgment and the ensuing new age.

In a second article, Klaus Bäumlin observes that apocalyptic literature "has been dusted off and is once again in vogue."[6] As the millennium approached, *apocalyptic* became a household code word for an idea unthinkable to earlier generations. For the first time in human history, people believed that the world might be destroyed and that it would happen quickly, not because of divine or cosmic intervention, but because of human action and/or neglect. Thus, this may be the age when "heaven and earth will pass away" (Matt 24:35).

This apocalyptic mood, promoted mightily by literalist readers of the Bible, has been so pervasive that it is found in contemporary books, movies, plays, and music. Apocalyptic consciousness has indeed permeated today's world, but has an attitude of hope prevailed?

Many people make false claims about apocalyptic literature, believing that it predicts the future at a specified time. Much of this concern has been highlighted by a fundamentalist view of the future, that God will use certain persons to assist in the destruction of evil and they alone will be the *saved*. All others will be condemned for their participation in evil and/or their refusal to cooperate with God in this destruction. Many innocent people have gotten caught up in the frenzy of the end-time phenomenon and, wishing to be among the saved, prepare for the time when God will "swoop down" and conquer all evil by becoming involved in these cults.

The literalist reading promoted by fundamentalist sects is not helpful for building the imagination of the general public, nor is it supportive of us as imaginative teachers and preachers. First, the literalist approach tends to rummage through apocalyptic texts in order to look for prophesies of specific events and apply them to today. This literalist approach involves poor exegesis and significantly ignores the historical context of the written text. Biblical texts had a specific meaning for a certain audience of the ancient literature. Readers today can apply them, but they cannot suppose they are living in the era for which the text was written. This literalist approach conveys a deterministic approach to history, symbolized by haughty Jonah sitting in the shade waiting for catastrophe to occur (Jonah 4:5–11). This method leaves little room for responsible faith action because it upholds that the world can't change, so why try. There is a loss of hope in this approach to reading apocalyptic literature.

We are not assisted by another prominent method, which can be termed the individualistic method. According to proponents of this reading style, metaphors and images primarily aid individuals on their personal quest for holiness. This approach contrasts sharply with an essential feature of apocalyptic texts: they highlight God and community more than a *me and God* approach to holiness. Of course, apocalyptic literature holds individuals accountable for their actions, but it offers hope by first addressing the community and seeking its benefit. People are called to community, forming a *people of God* who respond to God's covenant. If people regress into the stress on personal holiness, they tend to deny their membership in the body of the faithful, the hope-filled, covenant community. God calls people together to face the troubles of the world. It is together that they move hopefully toward the reign of God. When we use imagination in preaching and teaching, we must accent this communal dimension of the literature.

This book, then, encourages us to be confident by instilling a more intimate reflection upon the hopefulness of apocalyptic texts. The message of hope must be taught, imagined, and preached in all places and in all mediums, as it is revealed to us, both in prayer and in exegetical study.

LOOKING AHEAD

In chapter 1, the focal point is a basic definition of apocalyptic literature that we as preachers, teachers, and imaginative readers can grasp. This definition leads the reader into chapter 2, the heart of the book, which unmasks hope as that virtue most needed by those who attempt to preach and teach apocalyptic texts. This chapter sets the stage for the rest of the work by promoting an effective teaching and preaching of these texts by stretching our imaginations and encouraging us to offer a message of hope, especially to a struggling people eager to imagine hope in their lives.

Chapter 3 discusses the great importance of imagination in both teaching and preaching from apocalyptic literature. In order to use apocalyptic texts to teach or preach that hopeful message, we must be aware of the fact that we are reading crisis literature that gives hope through the imaginative destruction of evil.

The metaphor of unmasking used throughout the book is powerful for those who preach or teach apocalyptic literature because it opens our imaginations as we prepare to give an important message in the sermon or in the classroom. The Greek word apocalypse *(apokalepsis)* means "to unveil" and is synonymous with the image of unmasking. The question arises: Who or what is being unmasked? The texts when read by people of the biblical world were in no need of unmasking, for those readers usually knew what the images and symbols meant. But those same texts today are puzzling. Thus, both text and reader need unmasking in order to embrace these writings.

In order to assist the unmasking of the texts, a model is provided for thinking more deeply about apocalyptic literature in general. The concept of tragic drama is introduced in chapter 4 and a model from tragic theatre is adapted to apocalyptic literature in chapter 5. Apocalyptic literature is emphasized as that genre of scripture that engages dramatic imagination in order to offer hope when most needed. It proposes a message of indomitable hope in a God whose care for humans on their eternal quest knows no bounds! Drama, which enriches imagination, is thus an important and often overlooked element.

Continuing the unmasking of apocalyptic texts, chapters 6 through 10 investigate the apocalyptic texts of both testaments, with a three-step methodology. The first step unveils the historical situation of the community in crisis, while the second step overviews each apocalyptic text and indicates its relevance for unmasking hope from that crisis. Finally, step 3 gives practical assistance to those preaching from and teaching apocalyptic texts by suggesting themes from the overviewed text that focus a particular preaching or teaching and also identifying the function of that theme for a given use. The section concludes with a skeleton outline upon which to build that preaching or teaching. These outlines can also be utilized in classroom teaching by building a lecture from the theme and outline given for the various sermons.

A reckless approach that ignores good exegesis blossomed well before the year 2000. Hal Lindsey, in his book *The Late Great Planet Earth*, commanded the attention of millions with his biblically based prediction of the end times. This approach is an irresponsible reading of apocalyptic texts. However, Lindsey created many curiosity seekers, who magnified the apocalyptic phenomenon, asking "when" the end will be. These honest seekers probably inspired fundamentalist cult leaders who interpreted the Bible literally, thought of themselves as God's anointed fighters against evil, and prepared for the *when* of the end by building heavily armed shelters to ward off evil. Rather than rely on fundamentalist interpretation of the Bible, chapters 6 through 10 depend upon the results of historical-critical scholarship as well as narrative and social criticism.

Besides a lack of responsible exegesis, a certain mindset was exhibited as the world moved toward year 2000 that also indicates need for this book. The mass media captured this mindset in its extensive reporting of radical groups and their fear of the end time's phenomenon. Their approach highlighted the strange symbolic style of the literature and the theme of preparing for survival after the rapture. Where, in this scenario, was the possibility of apocalyptic literature as a word of hope *from* God or *about* God? In the end, the media reinforced the sense that perhaps those who fear apocalyptic literature are more prevalent than those who embrace these texts.

If fear is the prevailing response of the general public regarding this literature, then it is probably the same for many teachers and preachers. Statistical answers are not available as to whether we confront our fears of apocalyptic literature. Perhaps the media hype causes tension within some of our minds as we desperately try to read the signs of the times as part of our teaching or preaching preparation. This publicity may have caused fanatical groups to be so influential that they encourage us to question whether apocalyptic texts are viable for our teaching and preaching. Thus, we may neglect the opportunity to breathe the fresh air of eschatological hope by presenting apocalyptic symbolism as allusions to a future, hope-filled world related to the way humans live in the present world.

Chapter 11 returns again to the theme of hope by reflecting on how we are encouraged to move toward Christian actions with hope-filled eyes. It is important to use apocalyptic literature to increase our hope in order to live into the future that God has planned for us. The community element is especially stressed so that people learn to stand together in times of crisis. This chapter concludes by giving specific ideas about the use of apocalyptic texts prior to and during Advent, the season when they are most prominent in the lectionary. Advent and hope are synonymous.

Chapters 12 and 13 conclude this book by reflecting upon my personal journey toward hope. Chapter 12 speaks of the call that I experienced, a call away from violence and toward hope. This reflection grounds the entire book, discussing the elements that make up the preaching and teaching of apocalyptic literature that I have done. The chapter culminates with two sample preachings. Chapter 13 presents my theology of preaching. One can see in this chapter the inclusiveness that has permeated my life as I have lived into the message of the apocalyptic texts about which I write. Last, the Appendix gives the reader help in identifying apocalyptic texts with a table drawn from the various lectionaries of the liturgical cycle.

Before moving into the heart of this work, then, let us begin with a basic definition of apocalyptic literature that will ground the remaining chapters' approach.

We may never see the end results.
We are workers, not master builders,
ministers, not messiahs.
We are prophets of a future not our own.
—*Attributed to Oscar Romero*[1]

Chapter One

DEFINITION OF APOCALYPTIC LITERATURE

Scholars have had a great deal of ambivalence regarding apocalyptic literature. John Collins illustrates that ambivalence. On the one hand, he quotes Ernst Käsemann: Apocalyptic is "the mother of all Christian theology." On the other hand, he immediately cites Klaus Koch, saying, "Apocalyptic is perplexing and embarrassing."[2] Collins wisely reflects upon the embarrassing popular association of the word *apocalyptic* with fanatical millennial groups, who justify their actions in the name of a God who is intent on destroying evil and cautions against a prejudice that is pervasive even within biblical scholarship. He further suggests that overreaction as a result of such a one-sided approach characteristic of millennial groups is unwarranted and asks for restraint on the part of all. Scholars have more recently begun to open themselves more fully to the realization that the "apocalyptic myth"[3] does not always correspond to what is found in actual apocalypses.[4] Let us look more closely at how the theological prejudice has confused the imagining public as well as teachers and preachers.

Confusion among readers comes from the fact that they must clearly distinguish apocalyptic literature in its many forms as well as define various terms that may have been carelessly used.

Although it is noteworthy to speculate upon the number of works that are called apocalypses, especially since works of Jewish apocalyptic literature were not labeled as apocalypses in antiquity, it is important to realize that the Greek word *apokalepsis* [apocalypse = revelation] as a type of literature does not appear in the time before Christianity, but only comes to the fore very late in the first century.

Let us focus, then, on some of the categories of study. The all-encompassing term written about is "revelatory literature," with apocalypse becoming a subset of that general category. From this class of revelatory literature, it is possible to distinguish apocalypticism as a social ideology, apocalypse as a literary genre, and apocalyptic eschatology as a group of motifs that may also be found in other social settings and literary genres.

On the one hand, some scholars have implied that there is no distinctive apocalyptic eschatology and that focus upon that aspect within the general populace is unfounded. However, apocalyptic eschatology is an important dimension of this book. It is discussed here because the end of history is significant to the apocalyptic texts within the biblical literature.

On the other hand, apocalypticism is a historical movement referring to the symbolic universe where an apocalyptic movement codifies its identity and analysis of reality. As an example, this distinction embraces the sect of early Christianity (pre-70 CE) and also that of Qumran, a community commonly regarded as apocalyptic. These movements are generally included within apocalyptic literature because they endorse a worldview in which the heavenly world and eschatological judgment played indispensable parts and assisted people in imagining their future in an extremely positive manner.

Apocalyptic language is also an important concern, for the manner of composition and the nature of the literature are just as significant as the generic framework. Thus, significant debate continues as to whether or not apocalyptic literature is the child of prophecy or the child of the wisdom tradition. These distinctions cannot be ignored, but they can be left to scholars to determine. Those preparing a sermon or a teaching lecture need not be concerned with these distinctions.

It cannot be assumed that all apocalyptic literature was penned under a single movement and so it is essential to study the social settings of apocalyptic works. Apocalyptic movements emerged within the Jewish tradition as well as within fringes of Judaism (Qumran) and early Christianity. In most cases, it is fundamental to know that the social and historical setting for these texts involves the heat of persecution.

We preachers and teachers must also recognize that the pseudonymous authors of these symbolic texts frequently were scribes, who authenticated their claim to authority and gave credibility to their reported visions by writing under a well-known name rather than their own. That claim to authority allows the texts to be more acceptable. Thus, they are a product of learned activity that engages one's vivid imagination and are not to be dismissed by the preacher or teacher as unimportant, although popular, folklore.

After reading about the struggle to accept apocalyptic literature, we may be surprised that apocalyptic works were embraced within the canon of the scriptures. It seems that the only viable reason for their presence is the mysterious working of God's Spirit in producing the canon. This mystifying process and its accompanying technicalities, important as they are to scholars, allow for a clear definition that will offer guidance to those who encounter these texts in the lectionary or who choose them for a Sunday sermon or who wish to speak about them in a classroom. The following definition grounds this work:

Apocalyptic literature is a cluster of writings with a narrative framework intended for a group in crisis, addressing concerns regarding renewal of faith and reordering of life on the basis of a vision experienced by the seer. This revelation is mediated by an otherworldly being to a human recipient. The author tends to relativize the significance of existing realities by depicting how they are about to be superseded by God's universal reign. This transcendent reality is temporal in that it visualizes eschatological salvation as well as spatial because it involves a supernatural world. The eschatological event in question can neither be hastened nor thwarted by human efforts, but will unfold, true to an eternal plan, as a result of divine action.[5]

This comprehensive definition has five significant elements that the teacher and preacher must note. The literature:

1. Is intended for a group in crisis
2. Addresses renewal of faith and ordering of life
3. Involves a vision from an otherworldly being to a human recipient
4. Emphasizes God's universal reign rather than existing realities
5. Unfolds the eschatological event as a result of divine action

The core attribute that necessitates concern about an apocalyptic worldview is the presence of an otherworldly deliverer, usually an angel, who interprets the vision or serves as guide on the journey. Thus, some apocalyptic literature, for example the Book of Daniel, chapters 7–12, is surrounded by remoteness and mystery and presents a human recipient as a venerable figure from the distant past. This venerable figure indicates how the wicked will be destroyed so that a hope-filled final judgment of all persons and all reality takes place.

People cannot imagine such a world of hope unless they know what kind of life it calls them to lead. It is appropriate, then, for those who wish to embody hope as well as speak hope, to reflect upon its meaning. In chapter 2, the topic of hope is introduced.

Have patience with everything
that is unsolved in your heart.
Try to love the questions themselves.
Do not look for answers.
They cannot now be given to you
because you could not live them.
At present you need to live the question.
                    —*Rainer Maria Rilke*[1]

Chapter Two

WALKING TOWARD HOPE

Biblical texts in the various lectionaries near the Advent season are filled with apocalyptic imagery. They underscore warnings about *Jesus returning soon* and how people are called to *change their lives*. These texts are meant to bestow hope, but people often respond to them with anxiety because they are readying themselves for the "merry" season of Christmas. In the end, most people probably ignore these apocalyptic warnings as mere misplacement in the lectionary. However, if the preacher or teacher recognized the hope in these passages, they would be preached much differently. This chapter investigates the virtue of hope and encourages those who teach and preach apocalyptic literature and those who are required to preach in apocalyptic-like times to focus upon hope.

Two examples reinforce the significance of hope as more than a virtue for the Christmas season. A university chaplain begins student project meetings with this question: "What's your 100 percent for this project?"[2] Student responses give clarity to their ideal hope for a given venture. In this way, the chaplain moves students to deeply reflect upon the projects they suggest. Ideally, he hopes the students will view any plan from a larger perspective than that from which they originally suggested the plan. The chaplain wants the students to accomplish what they desire, but also have the projects benefit the total campus ministry program as well as the entire university.

In 1979, while Jimmy Carter was president, he had a remarkable experience of hope. An interviewer recently asked, "How did you maintain hope through the Iran hostage crisis?" Since the president and his advisors had not found a way to resolve the crisis, Carter recalled feeling extreme pain for the families who would have Christmas without loved ones. During the National Christmas Tree lighting, Carter was surprised by God's presence. His daughter Amy, honored to flip the switch, gasped along with the crowd when only the star at the top lighted. In the innermost part of his heart, Jimmy Carter calmly reflected that this "Star of Hope" was God's sign that "all would be well."[3]

Will *all be well* in our world? I submit that it will be difficult unless we learn to bring people hope in the midst of the crises that surround us every day. However, we cannot bring what we do not understand. In a workshop I gave a couple of years ago, I spoke of being a preacher and teacher of hope by using apocalyptic texts. A preacher declared to me at the end that he wondered if he brought hope to his people each week. I recommend every teacher and preacher who reads this book ask that same question. The reflection upon hope that follows assists us with this understanding.

THE PASSION OF HOPE

Saint Thomas Aquinas wisely begins with a reflection on the passion of hope, in order to help people grasp the meaning of the virtue. On the one hand, he notes that passion is a high-intensity movement of the appetite. On the other hand, he specifies that a low-intensity movement would be simply a feeling. Both movements encompass knowledge as well as some sort of psychic element. Ordinarily, with no obstacle present, an act of hope arouses the passion of hope.[4]

Ernst Bloch stresses that the emotion of hope goes out of itself by making people think more broadly without confining them and also makes them inwardly aimed but outwardly allied.[5] Thus, people of hope throw themselves actively into what is becoming.

We can conclude, then, that easily obtainable things are within people's power and do not require hope. Since no one strives after the impossible, hope, as a passion, is fundamental and basic to all human goals. We can also surmise that there is always a social value to hope. It is important to realize that, in connection with apocalyptic literature, hope resulting from apocalyptic literature is situated in the natural world while still retaining a supernatural value.

CAUSES OF HOPE

Hope has two fundamental causes: anything that makes things possible and anything that makes people consider something possible. Since hope arises when there exists uncertainty of attaining good, these causes depend upon the intellect. So, anything is a cause of hope that increases one's power to make things possible that may have been out of reach. For example, wealth can be a cause of hope because it makes possible so many difficult goods, which are not in the power of someone who is poor. It all depends upon how the wealth is used. The same can be said about education. Our United States Constitution describes education as an inalienable right. If that is true, why are we not working harder to make sure that every child has a quality education? As it is now, our educational system needs revamping in order to bring hope to many people.

Another aspect of hope is one's attitude. A person may embark on an enterprise without confidence, but while gaining experience will generate hope that the object is within reach. On the other hand, a given experience might cause a loss of hope if it destroys people's confidence and makes them judge that an undertaking will be impossible in the future. Healthy people usually have energy and vigor and thus may be more hopeful and daring in difficult actions or events. In the same way, the young usually have a more optimistic outlook because they have not tasted defeat, been conquered, nor suffered as many impediments in their efforts. In the end, those who live happily are more hopeful than those who live in sadness, for the latter tend to fall into despair much more easily. Also, trust in others and in divine providence leads one to daring hope. Thus, it is impossible to think of belief in God as a hindrance to energetic social action.

EFFECTS OF HOPE

The fundamental effect of hope is that it assists action. First, hope arouses attention, causing one to plan well and work tirelessly in order to bring about a given objective. When unanticipated obstacles block their achievement, hopeful persons will not be frustrated or overwhelmed. However, those who engage in activities without weighing the difficulties will be discouraged more easily.

Second, by bringing joy, hope intensifies a project and aids its completion. Greater joy will arise from the actual possession of a good. However, when one is not sure of obtaining that object, joy must spring forth from hope.

Third, when hope is passionate, that passion leads to an audacious readiness to attack evil. An intense hope is able to correct abuses and remove hazardous obstacles. Thus, those who are hopeful usually accept the burden of conquering the tribulations that threaten the welfare of society. These hopeful people allow a more optimistic future for all.

DESPAIR

Hope is appreciated more fully when it is weighed against its opposite—despair. If good seems impossible, fear may overwhelm him or her and they will eventually move into a state of sadness. Ultimately, the state of sadness leads to despair and increases the potential for fear. Thus, in order for those who are sad to move from fear, which is capable of plunging them into despair, they ought to make their goals very realistic. This will potentially allow the sad to try a task that will give them a sense of joy and hope.

THE SOCIAL VALUE OF HOPE

Social contentment is achieved when a large number of people desire a common goal and are willing to sacrifice for it. The amount of confidence that people have in their social reality increases their intensity of effort, hope, and enthusiasm. This fervor is able to thaw the cold of despair, which then spreads warmth and enthusiasm to those who are indifferent or lethargic. As an example, consider hope as a vital part of our educational program. Hope by a teacher allows a student to feel confidence. If educators do not have enthusiasm and hope in executing a program, it will fail and will cause frustration for all. Stability in education brings forth hope.

Hope is vital when a nation is at war for, if there were no unyielding hope of victory, that nation would already be defeated. Hope is also essential for a nation that embarks on the hazardous undertaking of making our world more peaceful. Without hope, international relations cannot be unwavering and harmonious.

THE SUPERNATURAL VIRTUE OF HOPE

The previous discussion of hope was on the purely natural plane. However, Aquinas indicates that the theological virtue of hope is something different. It is "a habit of will infused by God."[6] God is the actor, and we are God's instruments of salvation. Thus, this virtue spurs anticipation of eternal life and the confidence needed to move in that Godly direction. People must pray for the grace of hope, for no one can be admitted to eternal life by proxy.

As a theological virtue, the primary object of hope is an invincible God. Supernatural hope presupposes the grace of God, for the journey would be impossible without such grace. This grace differentiates hope from the moral virtues, which focus upon the regulation of human activity. Nevertheless, there is no complete separation, for hope is needed in the temporal realm as well.

Even though hope has God as its principal object, it is justifiable and even mandatory to hope in creatures as secondary causes.[7] Being in community with others, people can hope that their common faith will lead them toward God. Thus, authentic relationships are extremely important in the development of hope. These relationships depend upon unselfish giving, which leads them to share faith with others in the community. In order to be beneficial, then, hope is to be founded on true knowledge of self, others, and God.

Hope as an ideal has incredible magnetism and can inspire both resoluteness and zeal for good. We who are engaged in preaching and teaching are required to develop our own hope in a God who has always journeyed with us and will always be with us. If we are convinced teachers and preachers who present this ideal attractively, it can be a smoldering spark in the hearts of even the dullest people and may be fanned into flame.

Preachers and teachers of the book share a common hope that God will send a messiah to lead the way back to God.[8] This messianic hope commonly includes the following factors:

- Hope in a future condition of society in which peace and justice will prevail
- A chosen group by which this reign of justice is procured
- Religious fervor ignited by the conviction that a divine destiny is being fulfilled
- Reward for the suffering and sacrifice of the "chosen" after enemies are crushed
- A conviction and desire to spread peace and justice to others not so favored

Modern messianism can be traced specifically to the Jewish people who never lost hope, from their first covenant with God to the promise that God would be with them for all times. The Son of man (Dan 7:13) in apocalyptic literature, never identified and representing many different entities throughout the ages, is a glorious figure that, for those of the First Testament, will rescue the Jewish people from their own inability to live the covenant.[9] The ideal Son of man, the Messiah still expected among the Jewish people, will inaugurate a new era of religious and moral perfection.

Summarizing these aspects of hope will be helpful to those of us who preach and teach. Hope is:

- Knowledge of a future good, hard to obtain but possible
- A characteristic embraced by healthy people and by the young
- Achieved when one trusts in other people
- Fundamental to action and brings joy when the action is completed
- Achieved in a state of social contentment within a given community
- Personal in that each person ought to strive for hope
- A theological virtue of the will infused by God and thrusting one toward eternal life

CHARACTERISTICS OF HOPE

Eschatology (from the Greek *eschatos*, meaning "last") is a branch of theology whose focus is beliefs concerning death, the end of the world, and the ultimate destiny of humankind. Specifically, eschatology concerns the various doctrines regarding the coming of the Messiah, the resurrection of the dead, and the Last Judgment. It is interesting to note that this science of the last things has usually presupposed that God would never break into human history. This has had a sad result in that hope has often been forgotten as a virtue to be sought.

This neglect of hope needs to be turned around so that hope can become a virtue by which humanity lives in the *todays* of their existence. If such change does not happen, it will continue to rob humanity of hope that the promised Messiah would be critically significant for people in the *here and now*. For Jürgen Moltmann, the notion that God would never break into human history leads to a sterile subsistence, "like a loosely attached appendix that wanders off into obscure irrelevancies."[10]

This negative eschatological thrust has often left humanity at the mercy of inane thinkers who reformulated a definition of hope in contradiction to everyday experiences of evil, suffering, and death. This type of eschatology has cheated humans of happiness in this world, for as long as hope does not embrace and transform humanity's actions, it remains ineffective.

Moltmann reverses the discussion of hope by presenting it as the "foundation and mainspring of theological thinking."[11] In this view, the current world becomes important and humans can expect to be happy now *and* in the future. Essentially, Moltmann defined the *Parousia* (a Greek term for the end of historical time) as a *not yet* and a *now* phenomenon, which conceptualizes an imminent God impregnating time, then cutting the umbilical cord of the womb of eternity and birthing hope within humanity.

This picture declares the priority of faith but the primacy of hope. Clearly, without the mysterious knowledge that leads one to faith, hope hangs in the air as an ideal that is extremely complex and difficult to achieve. But, once humans have birthed the seed of God's future within themselves and within the world, they will be "restless until they rest in God."[12]

Nevertheless, the goal can still be unclear and extremely difficult to maintain. The good that leads to a promised future stabs relentlessly into the flesh of every disappointed present. Thus, it is impossible for people to achieve fullness of faith in God unless they overcome the necessary conflicts of existence in this imperfect world. Hope can so easily drift into despair when people attempt to shield themselves from disappointments, crises, and other evils.

Another aspect of hope to consider is that it can make fools of those who believe in God. Of course, humans ought to seek God's solace and compassion. At the same time, however, people must realize that they live in weakness, weariness, and timidity, not wanting to be what God requires of them. Humans may think they are growing closer to God because they have resisted the titanic desire to *be* God. Nevertheless, they may still abuse the beautiful creation that God provides. An emphasis on hope calls humanity beyond such recklessness and toward a faith-filled hope that is an inexhaustible resource for the inventive imagination of love. A hope that leads one to belief breaks the stalemate of existence and teaches humans to love the entire created world and others as well as themselves.

A believing hope leads a person toward an apocalyptic mentality, where he or she will be called to think in cosmological patterns beyond history while living faith out in the everyday. The wind of the Spirit will not allow history to stagnate but will intelligibly represent reality in its totality. Thus, the apocalyptic process splits the universe into two aeons: a world that is passing away and a world that is coming. Such a prophetic, apocalyptic journey calls forth conversion from humanity and correlates this change with the entire cosmos.

Theologian Michael Downey characterizes hope with two firm convictions:

1. There is nothing more central to being human than being able to hope.
2. Hope of the deepest kind can come only as a gift from God.[13]

The gift of hope comes to humans from God when they understand the shape of life with God. It is easy to lament the insidious loss of hope in today's postmodern world, with the young and the not-so-young wandering aimlessly, without a clear sense of commitment for building a preferred future. Perhaps that aimless wandering has to do with the evils of the twentieth century, which destroyed most presuppositions regarding human progress and shattered a seemingly unifying worldview. It seems that this postmodern era has a universal sense that people are incapable of constructing legitimate maps for an authentic future. However one looks at this postmodern world, it seems that one will be buoyed by writers, artists, and poets whose hints of hope have opened humanity to epiphanies, to the big picture of clues and insights that will guide humanity.

One thing is sure. There is an approach for constructing a reliable and coherent worldview without following those who call into question the existence of a loving God. On the one hand, an irreligious approach does not abandon hope but recognizes that humanity is extremely more fragile than it really is. On the other hand, those who are strong, yet vulnerable, are akin to those who sense the nakedness of their beings while still being able to call upon a strong, yet vulnerable, God to assist them in stirring up a new desire for hope.

I am convinced that people cannot live without hope because they would wander aimlessly without being committed to anyone or anything. The characteristics of hope they most need include patient waiting with immense openness toward the promised future, allowing hope to be the driving force that looks for the newness within that which has never been before. Recognizing hope as the great virtue of the human person *in via* (on the way), we finally look in expectation toward the Other in the realization that, if and when hope comes, it arrives totally as gift.

Of course, hope is gift, but why is it not seen that way? I suggest that people tend to use hope only as an emergency virtue. Thus, when a crisis occurs, their "disaster lights" are too dim to assist them in getting out of a difficult time. If hope is disregarded except during emergencies, humans lose the expectation of the present moment, the ability to move beyond this moment to the next with the gift of God's grace. Thus, the strength of hope shores up human energy to perform a task, not because there is some reward to be had, but because people realize that God is leading them in a new direction, which is building the reign of God with an enthusiastic and passionate vision.

Political scientist Glenn Tinder describes hope in a way that carries significance for understanding its fullness. The proper perspective is that hope is for God. Our nature as rational and questioning beings means that we can come to rest only in the presence of the infinite. Our transcendental reference points would be prologues to tragedy were it no more than a question spoken into the darkness. However, out of the dark night there comes a response. We hear the word of God, the *logos* (see John 1:1–4) in whatever language we best hear that and look for the light in order to see God.[14]

Last, a very simple way to accent hope is provided by Richard Fragomeni. Hope is *being surprised by God* in such a way that persons make new decisions that will allow them to be "fully human—fully alive."[15]

In order to provide a convenient reference for teachers, preachers, and imagining readers, the diverse characteristics noted in the analyses of the virtue of hope just completed are summarized in the succinct statements appearing in Table 1. These characteristics of hope provide impetus to walk through the scriptures and see how they embody and initiate hope.

Table 1. Characteristics of Hope

- Hope is the heart and center of the healthy human being.
- Hope is a theological virtue of the will infused by God.
- Hope begins with knowledge of a future good that is hard to obtain but possible.
- Hope buoys belief in God, for faith nourishes and sustains it.
- Hope is the great virtue of the human person *in via* (on the way).
- Hope is the dynamism that carries us forward from what is to what is still to come.
- Hope is an immense openness to and expectation of gift, a future promised by God.
- Hope is resting in God, the infinite, and the eternal.
- Hope grows when one trusts other people, but it is also very personal.
- Hope always looks for newness, what has never been before but is only for God.
- Hope is a positive response to a negative darkness.
- Hope is being surprised by God.
- Hope cares tenderly for a devastated Earth, not allowing its contamination.
- Hope is the original impulse of our natural, questioning, patiently waiting beings.
- Hope matures in a state of social contentment within the community.
- Hope is hearing God's word and seeing the light of God's promise.
- Hope always lives in the vale of earthly tears but moves toward God who quickens that difficult journey.

HOPE IN THE FIRST TESTAMENT SCRIPTURES

The fire of truth contained in the Second Testament is built upon the flaming embers of the First Testament. These embers cannot be extinguished, for the deep truth of God's promise forms the foundation for all the hopes of the future.

The nomadic religion of the Israelite people is a religion of promise. God's name discloses a new future, whose truth is experienced in history.[16] We are invited to journey with the people of the first covenant and discover the hopeful promises contained in the stories of Israelite history.

The story of God choosing a people with whom to journey and promising that they would be God's people forever is the basis of hope for those who embrace the scriptures as their own story. Throughout the Hebrew scriptures, a steady pattern of promise gave the chosen people hope that God was with them:

- An individual hears a promise from God.
- The people accept that promise and make a covenant with God.
- The people act against the promise.
- God becomes angry with the people.
- A person intercedes to God for the sinful people.
- God relents and renews the covenant promise with the people.

Whoever wrote these scriptures belonged to a community that learned of God's faithfulness through many trying times. In telling this story, the writer records many difficult times when the Israelites learned the same lesson the hard way. The lesson of the journey with God is the venerable task of replacing stony hearts with natural hearts (Ezek 36:26).

The most significant text describing this First Testament pattern is the exodus from Egypt:

- Moses hears God's promise in a burning bush to care for the people (Exod 3:3ff).

- The people respond that they will always follow God's way (Exod 19:7–8).
- The weary people construct a molten calf and dance around it (Exod 32:1ff).
- God becomes angry with the people (Exod 32:7–10).
- Moses intercedes to God for the people (Exod 32:11–14).
- God relents and the people renew their covenant with God (Exod 32:34).

The memory of the exodus and the covenant on Sinai spurred the Israelites forward. The living out of the exodus journey reminded the scholars of the scriptures to pen the rest of the story. Most Jewish people relive that exodus journey each year during the celebration of Passover, which is a time of hope and promise, a time to experience again God's faithfulness and love. This Exodus pattern is the starting point for a journey of conversion and hope.

This scriptural journey is absurd for some, but life giving for many others. On the one hand, the philosopher Albert Camus did not find the exodus theme helpful as a metaphor for promise by God, but rather for the estrangement from God. For Camus, the exodus "referred to the condition of humanity in the absence of God."[17] Possibly for others as well, exodus was thought to be an image of exile without remedy, with no memory of a lost home or any hope of a promised land. Thus, Camus encouraged others to create their own meaning by revolting against their condition, taking the stance that they were stronger than their human condition.

On the other hand, the First Testament's promised exodus of deliverance in the midst of human weakness is meaningful for those who have faith nourished by hope. Since their spiritual lives are based upon scripture, they read it with an open heart and thus find a loving God who moves before and with the chosen people. God's hope-filled promise continues with the same Exodus pattern in the text about Abraham and Sarah:

- Abraham hears God and encourages Sarah to leave their home for a place God promises (Gen 12:1).

- God promises to be with Abraham's family *in via* (Gen 12:7–9).
- Abraham and Sarah long for the promised child and become discouraged (Gen 15:1–3, 16:1–6).
- God becomes angry with Sarah for laughing (Gen 18:13–14) and with Abraham for calling Sarah his sister (implied in Gen 12:10–15 and again in Gen 20:1–6).
- Abraham asks to be forgiven and is willing to sacrifice his son (Gen 22:1–14).
- God renews the covenant with Abraham (Gen 22:15–19).

Again, God's promise of faithfulness upholds David:

- David hears God's word and offers to build God a "house" (2 Sam 7:1–3).
- God promises to care for David and his inheritance (2 Sam 7:4–29).
- David murders Uriah in order to commit adultery with Bathsheba (2 Sam 11).
- God becomes angry at David (2 Sam 12:1–12).
- David himself intercedes before God for forgiveness (2 Sam 12:13–24).
- God renews the covenant through Solomon (1 Kgs 2:1–4).

The pattern of hope-filled promise continues, even though the Assyrians destroy the Northern Kingdom and send the people into deportation. Because the kings of Judah refuse to learn from their northern neighbors, eventually Judah, the Southern Kingdom, is also thrust into exile. However, the same blueprint of promise is also present throughout this critical time, with Ezekiel speaking God's loving presence to a people in a foreign land who felt abandoned by God (Ezek 1–3).

The hope-filled pattern of God's ardent love for the people is repeated in the work of many prophets. God never dismisses the covenant people because of sin but is very patient, taking them back again and again. That same hope-filled promise appears in the apocalyptic writings, which indicate a blurring of the promise in the midst of suffering. The historical present becomes a bridge to the eschatological future through the language of promise. Apocalyptic situations indicate passive resistance to powers opposed to God. In many cases, all that remains is martyrdom and suffering.

Faithful death in the early church was the only way to remain authentic for God. In today's world, many in Latin America have also suffered martyrdom. In the United States, where this is very seldom experienced, many must bear the lessons of suffering in other ways. Much of the work of God throughout the Bible is to get people into "liminal space," a place of suspension, and to keep them there long enough so they can learn essential realities.[18] This anomaly is the ultimate teachable moment because it drives one by the Spirit into the wilderness (see Mark 1:12).

For ordinary believers today, Lent can be the time when they choose liminality, when they choose to connect with the chaos of the unconscious and leave behind the control of explanations and answers.[19] As the early martyrs experienced the darkness of suffering, so, too, the Lenten readings present the language of darkness and desert. People need lessons in order to live in that uncontrollable place. Using the Moses image (Exod 3:5), one must be cautious, for darkness and desert is always holy ground where we are beckoned to take off our shoes before the presence of God. It takes a long time to learn to walk shoeless, probably symbolic of the fact that people don't want to stay on the threshold without answers.

Eschatological reflections in the apocalyptic readings juxtapose the hope-filled promise of God's continuing love with the stark realization that good will always overcome evil. God is still present with that same Exodus pattern in these readings as well:

- Daniel, whether legendary or not, was a "hero of God" (1 Macc 2:60).
- God was with Daniel in all his heroic ventures (Dan 1–6, 13–14).
- The people of the historical time associated with Daniel, the time of the Seleucid king Antiochus IV Epiphanes, often apostatized against their Jewish religion and took on Hellenistic practices (1, 2 Macc).

- Daniel intercedes with God for the chosen people; he has dreams that show the terror of the "beast" Antiochus IV Epiphanes and preaches them in order to set the people aright (Dan 7–12).
- The righteous ones renew their covenant with God, often in blood (Dan 7:18).

Israel's gift of promise was never liquidated, for newer and wider promises were reinterpreted through their experience of history. This broad application of apocalyptic hope continues for many with the texts of the Second Testament, the Christian scriptures, some of which are highlighted in the following section.

HOPE IN THE SECOND TESTAMENT SCRIPTURES

The hope of the Second Testament is of a different nature from that of the First Testament. Because many would say that the entire Second Testament was written in the shadow of an imminent *Parousia*, the color of the Second Testament is painted with hues of hope throughout, even though these messages are not particularly identified as apocalyptic texts.

The story of Paul recorded by Luke in Acts of the Apostles introduces the hope of this early, emergent church. In his constant defenses before the various tribunals of the Romans, Paul notes that it is his hope in God based upon the resurrection of Jesus that puts him on trial (Acts 24:15, 26:6). Ironically, Paul bases his defense also on his Jewish heritage. He preaches that his hope is based upon a hope that the Jewish people themselves also accept—that there will be a resurrection of both the righteous and the unrighteous (Acts 24:15). He also establishes his innocence on the fact that the Twelve Tribes of Jewish ancestry also prayed earnestly in hope day and night. Thus, Paul is stunned that his hope is the reason for the accusation by the Jewish leaders (Acts 26:7). Lastly, Paul, taken in chains to the emperor in Rome, establishes his innocence by indicating that it is *for the sake of Israel* that he is bound in chains (Acts 28:20).

That remarkable Lukan story gives justification for the many passages in Paul's letters that contain a message of hope. Paul regularly tells the story of his Jewish faith by relying upon the hope of his ancestors (see Rom 4:18). He also tells us that we ought to boast of our hope for the sake of the glory of God (see Rom 5:2). Paul admits that endurance produces character, that character produces hope, and that hope will never disappoint us (Rom 5:4–5). Paul also urges us to rejoice in hope (Rom 12:12) for, relying upon the First Testament, he says that "by the encouragement of the scriptures," we will have hope (Rom 15:4).

In a Letter to the Corinthians, Paul expresses his great hope for the people of that community. He admits that his hope for them is unshaken because they also share in his sufferings (2 Cor 1:7) and will be rescued from the deadly peril only if they have set their hope on the fact that Jesus will rescue them again and again (2 Cor 1:10). The Letter to the Ephesians exclaims that these early communities were the first to set their hope on Christ and, thus, they must live in the praise of his glory (Eph 1:12).

The more universal letters of the later church also boldly proclaim their trust in God because of the hope given them by Jesus the Christ (1 Pet 1:21). They are reminded to keep themselves pure to show the utter hope they have (1 John 3:3). Finally, the writer of Hebrews cautions the communities of faith to "hold fast to the confession of hope without wavering" (Heb 10:23), for God who gave the promise is always faithful. The final picture of hope (Rev 21) is the crowning glory of the Second Testament. The Book of Revelation gives an imaginary depiction of the destruction of all evil and the reign of glory that God had planned from the very beginning.

The promise? Yes, the writers of the early church spoke clearly of their belief in the promise of the First Testament. In a sense, this journey through the scriptures has come full circle. The promise of the First Testament leads to the hope expressed by the early Christians and that hope is justified because of their ancestors' belief in the promise.

We are called to proclaim in hope that God has given us the promise as well and that God will always be faithful. That eternal promise drives the apocalyptic writers of both testaments to express in stark, hopeful, and awesome ways that God will ultimately destroy all evil. Before we move to the exegetical analysis of those texts, however, readers will be introduced to the role of imagination in the understanding of apocalyptic literature.

Imagination is
the dancing partner of faith,
the guide into the unknown,
the source of creativity.
                    —*Ted Loder*[1]

Chapter Three

IMAGINATION AND APOCALYPTIC LITERATURE

While reflecting upon the nature of apocalyptic literature, Walter Brueggemann writes, "Much of our study of apocalyptic has been wrong-headed. We are too analytical, when in fact apocalyptic is literature asserting life finally ends in praise."[2] The "praise" theme reflects the fact that the world's reign will become the reign of God when all evil is destroyed. God shall reign forever and ever.[3] This chapter will be right-headed, focusing on the imagination needed in order to properly read apocalyptic literature. This imagination leads one to praise of God for God's great gift of salvation.

THE IMAGINARY PREACHER, TEACHER, AND READER

An essential responsibility of people on the path to the divine is the active utilization of all faculties entrusted to them. Indeed, the journey toward God cannot be passive! Imagination is one of those God-given faculties, and this powerful tool's potential for preaching and teaching ought to be explored.

Imagination, however, is hard to define. In the quote that begins this chapter, Ted Loder describes imagination as the "dancing partner of faith, the guide into the unknown [and] the source of creativity."[4] It is the way our dreams are silhouetted and it gives us a foretaste of our actions. It is a principal agent of truth and interpretation. It is more evocative and interpretive than factual and self-evident. Finally, it is an invitation to commitment, searching, and incarnation.

Dancing partner, guide, source—these describe imagination with strength and action. They assist in unmasking the journey toward God. Imagination is a creative activity that utilizes language polarities to generate fresh ideas. This creativity assists us who preach and teach to dream of our future with God and God's future with us. It sensitizes us deeply to how God is continually creative.

It is interesting that feminist theologians sometimes write of God as creativity. This embodiment of God is seen as enduring and dynamic activity. Thus, a stimulating implication of this view is that God seizes us through the experience of our own creativity and the exercise of our imagination.

This description of imagination is what apprehended the apocalyptic writers. They used their imaginations to symbolize the struggle of good over evil. Their creativity peaked while describing the eventual end of all evil and the hopeful movement toward that future God has planned for all creation.

Apocalyptic writers freed their imaginations by asking questions about God and about evil. In the broad sweep of life, questions are more crucial than answers for living well. We are propelled forward as we continually ask life to play its way toward its ultimate reward. This takes a great deal of patience and a loving spirit in molding our imaginations to live with questions. Then gradually, and without even noticing it, we find ourselves experiencing the possibility of an answer, however far distant that may be. For the apocalyptic author, God is the eventual answer and the only answer.

In order to become more effective preachers and teachers of the exciting and imaginative biblical apocalyptic passages, it is essential to rediscover the power of imagination. Yes, imagination can be experienced again. It is not a mystical experience to be avoided or feared. Well-trained, yet imaginative, teachers and preachers will be more disposed to conveying the word that God wants delivered to the people.

Paul Scott Wilson uses a Hebrew concept, imagining the heart as reconciler of our hearts as well as our head and our body as well as our mind in order to discern God's purpose. Wilson coins the phrase "imagination of the heart" for this experience.[5] For the Hebrews, the heart was the motivator of their entire spiritual lives, the seat of the emotions, intellect, and will. Thus, this Hebrew sense of heart comes very close to the ground of our being.

The heart image is not accidental. It is the language of poetry that leavens the teacher's and preacher's imagination. We, completely attuned to God's Spirit, allow that Spirit to touch our hearts at the core of our beings and move our imagination toward an image that has to be preached, that has to be taught. Thus, our preaching and teaching is shaped, molded, and composed—in a sense, even choreographed—by God's dance.

Under the direction of God's Spirit, the preaching/teaching moves and grows within us, uniting our minds with our hearts. The U.S. bishops' letter, *Fulfilled in Your Hearing*, stresses creative imagination by reminding preachers that the more we can turn to the graphic language of the poet and storyteller, the more we will be able to invite people inside the preaching so that they respond "from the heart as well as the mind."[6]

Such an inspiring and imaginative preaching/teaching allows listeners to reimagine theology in a way that will help them appreciate both experience and scripture. The process assumes that the poetic image has ignited a "spark" by placing the biblical text in tension with the existing situation. The flow chart in Figure 1 shows how, through the "spark" of tension, the preaching or teaching becomes an important vehicle for action, especially toward peace and justice. We do not ask if the image can be realized. Instead, we pray that the spark of tension we have purposely created through the use of certain images be released upon the community, who will then carry it to realization.

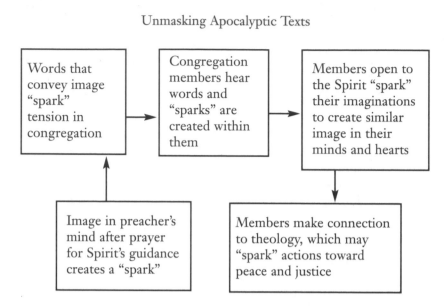

Figure 1. Preaching/Teaching with Sparks of Tension

In a similar way, the apocalyptic writer creates a spark of tension through the use of multiple images that represent biblical truths. See, for example, Ezekiel 1:15–21, where the living creatures from the Temple of God in Jerusalem are wheeled into Babylon so that the people again realize that God is present. A Second Testament example is Jesus' use of parables that, from the standpoint of imagination, create a spark by connecting story to religious idea.

The fundamental principle of the field of semiotics is that all meaning is relational. This basic principle is illustrated when, while teaching or preaching, we allow a metaphor to make a point. A vibrant example used by the poet-preacher Fred Buechner illustrates such a metaphor. He describes a rich person entering the realm of God as "a Mercedes going through a revolving door."[7]

The metaphor used may come from a careful word study, which may assist us to discover that word's root meaning. This may then allow us to open up a new range of thoughts and feelings within our imaginations. A metaphor may also emerge from a song or a poem, a recent movie, or a newspaper article. When we find a metaphor within the present stress of life's circumstances, we as creative teachers and preachers release the tension with images that allow that anxiety to be looked at more seriously.

Imagination blossoms when we learn to relax our "itchy fingers" that may wish to switch biblical channels too quickly. A raw encounter with the word of God, for example, allows a story image either to flow from the biblical text or to be found within the preacher/teacher. That story image is investigated for its multiple meanings, an essential step for igniting that imaginative spark between text and preacher or teacher.

If we seem blocked from finding an image, we may wish to experience the story of scripture by telling and retelling it as part of our preaching or teaching preparation. Only after all the imaginary embers are stoked do we turn to homiletic sources for igniting the idea already imaged. Imagination is crippled when we rush immediately to commentaries to get the correct answer, which we then regurgitate to our congregations or classes.

Imaginative preparation of any sermon or teaching necessitates literary analysis of the biblical text. This storylike method of analysis recognizes that any reader of the biblical text will always be full of questions. While preparing our preaching or teaching, it is important to think in the mode of the readers of our communities and the questions they have of the given text. If we begin preparation by thinking that the present is separated from both past and future, the questions coming from our experience of the community may be obstructed from our view.

The value of preaching and teaching from apocalyptic texts is that we are required to ask questions of both the past through memory and the future through imagination. Once we engage the apocalyptic text through questions, we then decide upon which question will focus a given sermon or class. Harnessing imagination and allowing the selected question to guide us will enhance the apocalyptic, prophetic ministry of the preacher or teacher. Of course, there are times when we cannot preach/teach prophetically, for listeners are not ready to hear the prophetic voice. Nevertheless, we can always use an imaginative approach to prepare ourselves, which assists the community to move toward readiness.

We are obliged to resurrect imagination in order to revitalize those words of faith that have lost their impact. According to Edward Markquart, most resident churchgoers do not have a gut association with key words of theology such as *salvation, incarnation, redemption, the cross,* and *resurrection.*[8] This glaring reality means that we must dare to gather up these theological words and allow the Spirit to blow through them, separating death-dealing theology from that which is life giving. This retrieval of meanings potentially offers new life to the laity who may use other words to speak about their everyday God-experience.

We end where we began. The journey toward God is constantly active, for God is always the dancing partner of faith. God guides each of us into the unknown of our own creativity, so that we will be able to use our faculty of imagination. In that way, God's word may be effectively and credibly preached or taught with innovative vision in an ever-changing world.

PREACHING AND TEACHING WITH AN IMAGINATIVE HEART: EXAMPLE 1

On February 10, 1999, as the culminating event of Black History Month, Brian Massingale, Professor of Systematic Theology at Xavier University in Milwaukee, warned the faith community at the Aquinas Institute of Theology that his talk would be disturbing, provocative, and inspiring, all at the same time. The audience stirred. Some felt curious, while others wiggled uncomfortably in their chairs. A few even walked out.

Massingale highlighted the fact that more than three hundred Internet Web sites promote hate crimes against African Americans by using the word *Negro* in an inflammatory way. This, he said, is the sign of our times from an African American perspective. His analyses of racism in light of faith were evocative. Stressing his pride that the Catholic Church has spoken out against racism, he defined racism with a statement from the national bishop's document *Brothers and Sisters to Us* as a radical evil that divides the human family. He also quoted John Paul II's indictment of racism. Speaking to an audience in St. Louis, Missouri (January 1999), John Paul II said that racism is one of the most persistent and destructive evils of our nation. According to the Holy Father, progress would not be made until racism becomes an American Issue.

Despite the panoply of disturbing statistics and provocative examples, Massingale was inspiring. He encouraged the audience to sustain a sense of hope in the midst of social actions. People can often feel rejected and discouraged, unless they realize that hope is generated through their understanding that they cannot save themselves. God alone saves. It is people's responsibility to believe that God alone saves and then to act as if God saves. Massingale warned against equating hope with optimism. Instead, he pointed toward hope as a radical trust in the faithfulness of God.

In a liturgy that followed, doctoral student George Franklin gifted the community with the experience of an excellent African American sermon. Preaching to a majority with European ancestry, Franklin asked the congregation to open their Bibles. After a short pause, he burst out in laughter. George knew from experience that most Anglos are not "Bible toters."

Both preachers were warm and expressive to the Aquinas community and spoke with their entire beings, not only their intellects. Reared in black cultural contexts, both were taught to call upon God in the throes of crisis and learned early that culture affects awareness and openness to faith. From my perspective, it was fascinating that the community seemed to react with a certain nostalgia for this type of worship.

As exemplified in these two guests to the Aquinas community, African American preaching and teaching comes from a heart of imagination that gives voice to God-given thoughts. Imagination sustained black persons in slavery as they found a parallel for their experiences in the Bible. They sang of their slave experiences as if the journey was happening all over again—out of Egypt with Moses to the Promised Land. They reveled in the baby Jesus who was *their* Messiah, even though most artistic expressions portrayed an Anglo baby Jesus. They raised the dry bones that resulted from the injustice they experienced.[9] Their storytelling and singing expressed their heart's imagination that God was a beloved parent to them all.

PREACHING AND TEACHING WITH AN IMAGINATIVE HEART: EXAMPLE 2

A second illustration comes from Thomas Troeger, who speaks clearly about the need for this kind of imagination among all preachers and teachers, not only among African Americans. He calls for believers to experience religious services as if they are stuck in a God-shaped hole and need to crawl out. This metaphor suggests the collapse of the dome of meaning, which happens when believers are faithful but think they fully understand God. Troeger laments this experience as the history of faith, a history of God-shaped holes.[10]

Today the world of the preacher/teacher is challenged by an unmistakable incompleteness of belief, a God-shaped hole. A new imagining is needed in order to find the application of God's word in a world living as if upon an earthquake. We must be institutional realists as we come to terms with new paradigms that give shape to the walking grace of the future church while still living in a present unsettled grace. Looking back in history is a way of relaying hope to today's gathering of believers, showing them that every time the biblical people's image of God crumbled, the wind blew and the Spirit stirred prophet or poet to preach a more expansive understanding of God.

Imaginative power is imperative in this world of conflicting images. The African American preachers modeled the kind of faith that holds strong while reconstruction of the church continues to take place. The apocalyptic task is the same, always wrestling with change. In like manner, apocalyptic writers remind the community that a tradition exists that supplies many of the materials essential for reconstructing the church for a new century. The visionary role of today's preacher of apocalyptic literature gives witness to an imaginative God who will revitalize both faith and ministry.

Social tensions between good and evil are the principal concerns of apocalyptic authors. Today's communities of faith need prophetic preachers and teachers willing to wrestle with those tensions in the hope of bringing forth a word from God. This is not easy, and it takes self-actualized persons to be this bold. One can feel leery about preaching or teaching in a prophetic way for two reasons:

1. Some listeners might challenge the preacher/teacher and express their distaste for prophetic preaching or teaching that integrates theology with politics.
2. Some may not understand that avoiding politics is, in itself, making a political statement.

Nevertheless, the day has come when more and more of us are required to become prophetic preachers and teachers. The 9/11[11] attacks on the World Trade Center and the Pentagon and their aftermath within the political arena are one sign that teachers and preachers today are required to speak prophecy to a world seeking retaliation rather than justice. We who have learned to stretch our imaginations before crises occur will be more capable of making credible prophetic statements in times of crisis. Imagine a church that is always a megaphone to the world and never a mere whisper!

Looking backward into church history assists us to realize that the church has always been under construction. Many essentials that are held dear today grew out of periods of theological turmoil. Effective preachers and teachers who lived in the fragmented world of their time presented the word of God with the visionary power they embodied. We today are called to do the same.

The Judeo-Christian tradition, as well as more ancient religious traditions, represents both an anchor and a cloud of witnesses. Like the anchor, solidified in mud, tradition holds us in place while the biblical text parades before us the cloud of witnesses, forming and reforming with the play of light and wind. This cloud of witnesses has always prepared humanity for the prophet, the one who faced the violent society in which they lived. That continues to happen today, for we are called to listen to prophets of peace.

We speak prophecy when we show that biblical references to violence are not from God, but were statements from a people who interpreted the belief that God would care for the people by destroying their enemies. We must preach and teach a gospel of grace, not feed people with violence. Interpretations that have attempted to explain away violent language as a hyperbole leave its use to fanatical believers with evil motives.

Reconstruction by today's biblical teacher and preacher of apocalyptic literature utilizes theological imagination. We who preach for a new millennium must be:

- Courageous
- Honest about the Bible's limitations
- Aware that the Bible, while divinely inspired, is not God
- Visionary risk-takers with new understandings of faith[12]

The new, imaginative, biblical preachers and teachers, modeling ourselves after our brother and sister African American preachers, will continue the work of theological renovation that each new God-shaped hole requires.

This work will probably be extremely dangerous for us, because it may awaken political and hierarchical resistance while challenging authority. Tradition is very clear: some people are stoned, crucified, and silenced when they become prophets against societal institutions in their teaching or preaching. Among First Testament prophets, Jeremiah's suffering because of his preaching is clear (see Jer 20:7–18). Also, Ezekiel suffered greatly as a watchman in exile (see Ezek 4). In the Second Testament, see Acts 7 for the stoning of Stephen and the numerous references in Acts and the letters about Paul's treatment because of his teaching and preaching.

The ultimate goal of visionary, prophetic preaching and teaching is imaginative accuracy. One utilizes the spark from the creative work that emerges in the gap between realities that initially seem unrelated—the biblical text and the teacher's or preacher's context. The sparks of imagination may run wild unless we, visualizing abstraction while employing the heart of tradition, solidify the preaching/teaching with discipline. That discipline usually emerges when we draw upon our personal experience as a source of spiritual energy and then use the God-shaped hole to revitalize our faith in God as well as our faith in the community.

We who preach and teach today can learn valuable lessons from our African American brother and sister preachers/teachers. Among the new insights are that African Americans preach and teach by using the Exodus story to create safety from the meaninglessness of racial oppression. They also paint eloquent pictures and use imaginative storytelling to connect themselves to the community's witness. Last, African American preachers and teachers discipline themselves by creating communal expectations within the community of being lifted out of sorrow.

Thus, the God-shaped hole provokes, disturbs, and inspires preaching and teaching. It generates hope that allows all brothers and sisters to be attentive to the walking grace of faithful living. It leads this writing to a place of excitement, where the reader is prepared for opening him- or herself to the way that drama is connected to apocalyptic literature. That is the subject of the next two chapters.

The Bible is not a reference book
so much as a book of clues in a treasure hunt.
It opens new areas for exploration
rather than closing life off behind
a fence of infallible answers.
                    —*Ted Loder*[1]

Chapter Four

TRAGIC THEATRE
AND CRISIS

AN EXPERIENCE WITH DRAMA

Drama has been a limited but important part of my life. Miming the gospel narratives together with narrators and musicians has been the most common dramatic medium. This miming is like praying, so that often persons lose themselves in their character when performing. Considering that none of the performers were professionals, the appreciative audience reaction has been surprising. Again and again, after the mime experience, someone in the audience expressed amazement and a prayerful sense of inspiration and meaning. A few comments include:

- "This was so powerful. I am stunned. The Gospel of Mark comes alive in a unique way."[2]
- "I get it now. I am supposed to be Jesus today!"[3]
- "Being involved in this mime prayer is like preaching."[4]

Recently, an acting class confirmed the same dramatic instincts discovered in the mime productions. Chris Limber, actor and teacher, modeled the integration between *doing* and *being* using specific exercises. As with miming, I found that it is necessary to be extremely comfortable with our bodies in order to be immersed in the part. This drama was experienced so that I could invite teachers and preachers of apocalyptic literature to look more closely at the dramatic event.

THE CONNECTION OF DRAMA TO APOCALYPTIC LITERATURE

Since ancient apocalyptic literature emerges in a time of crisis, it might be helpful to begin this exploration of drama by considering the form of drama called *tragedy*, which highlights the crises of history and suggests possible resolutions.

In his theory of drama, the Greek philosopher Aristotle exemplified the role of crisis in drama. He defined a dramatic tragedy as "a *mimesis*[5] of an action, morally serious and purposeful having magnitude; uttered in heightened language—[and bringing about] through pity and fear the purification of those destructive or painful acts."[6] Aristotle specified further that a tragedy is a *mimesis* not of people, but of life's actions. Therefore, plot has primacy over character.

Aristotle was thorough, assisting actors to understand what tragic drama was all about. He specified six aspects of the *mimesis*: two aspects of matter (speech and thought), one aspect of method (plot), and three aspects of subject (characters, staging, and song-making).[7]

He noted that the plot of the dramatic tragedy is always resolved at the end, for what matters is how the drama culminates. Within the plot, the drama engages the audience's heightened feelings with unexpected reversals and recognitions. However, recognitions are not as emotional as reversals because they work through signs, which indicate a poverty of imagination.

On the one hand, a sign can be "a gesture used to convey an idea, a desire, information or a command" but it may also be "a displayed structure bearing lettering or symbols."[8] Therefore, a sign is concrete and visible and, when utilized, imagination is not important.

On the other hand, a symbol cannot in itself be pictured, so it needs imagination to make it come to life. The language of symbol specifies areas of religious experience that are not accessible to purely theoretical reasoning but that have a genuine value for the expression of truth.

Aristotle also indicates that the poet, unlike the historian, is a true artist who can engage the reader's heightened imagination in a tragic poem. Whereas the historian tells what happened, the poet tells things that *can* happen. On the one hand, the historian deals with the particulars of time, geography, event, and so on. On the other hand, the poet deals with the universals of symbol, imaginative event, and dream.

Like the artist, the plot of the apocalyptic writer brings about a purification of painful acts that are resolved only in the end by a God who loves. The reader has heightened feelings while experiencing a particular dramatic event and ought to get beyond a poverty of imagination to appreciate this literature. Like the tragedian, the apocalyptic writer universalizes a particular crisis so that people of all ages may find life's actions within that crisis. Victor Turner's observation regarding literary genre applies also to apocalyptic: "Once a genre has become prominent, it is likely to survive or be revived at some level of the socio-cultural system, perhaps moving from the elite to the popular culture or vice-versa, gaining and losing audiences and support in the process."[9] Apocalyptic literature has been that way throughout the ages, being revived in some periods more than others as acute crises surfaced for the Hebrew people, within early Christian communities and even today.

THE DRAMATIC EVENT

Referring to both men and women, the actor's ultimate task is to enliven, to put together, and to create an experience of life in a fulfilling theatrical experience. Acting has great power. It may move, dazzle, charm, astonish, frighten, delight, and totally engage an audience. Acting has strength at the same time that it uses wit and grace, depth and openness. It can be the basis of true relaxation. Within the context of a dramatic event, a real but different universe exists. This new cosmos frees everyone—actor, playwright, and audience—to see and think differently, to ask new and different questions about life.

A highly structured dramatic event (for example, tragic theatre) can become a crucible that intensifies everything within it. This intensity implies that, most of the time, both participant and engaged observer are experiencing vivid action, which might at times be overwhelming. Actors become characters on stage in such a way that the audience experiences real persons who intensely act out real-life scenes. In that way, the dramatic event comes alive as it reveals, enlightens, and crystallizes life. Thus, drama hinges acting to reality. Otherwise, both drama and reality are diminished.

The dramatic event is more dynamic as the audience gets involved. They sit on the edge of their seats, waiting for performers to delight them with their characters. A significant facet of the acting experience is to enjoy, with your character, the pleasure of the moment. Thus, even though actors may not realize this, the play has enabled them to fulfill goals stemming from basic human instincts of survival, happiness, love, and validation. The focus on the artists' overall experience takes second place to the strong emphasis on their attitudes. When actors feel they have sincerely created the life of their characters, the audience usually responds appreciatively.

Before the performance, while exploring the character's past, these artists of the theatre express delight as they recreate the vagueness of a character's elusive present. In that way, the characters always progress during the performance. Acting involves a certain transformation that results in a focus of what actors *play into*, not what they *play out of*. Consider, for example, Walter Matthau's approach to playing a detective in *Twilight Walk*: Matthau is a human being who just happens to be a detective.[10]

In Cohen's theory of acting, there is an essential distinction between deterministic thinking (past-oriented, every action the result of a preceding action) and cybernetic thinking (future-oriented, dwelling upon complex systems that cannot be frozen for analysis). Actors are advised to exhibit cybernetic thinking, which always thrusts them toward the future while they act their characters out in the present.[11] Cohen offers three key reminders that serve to focus the actor's attention on cybernetic thinking:

1. Seek the purpose rather than the causes of your character's behavior.
2. Do not ask, "Why?" Ask, "What for?"
3. The character is "pulled" by the future, not "pushed" by the past.[12]

Those acting with authentic vitality will look to the past only to ask themselves the necessary questions about the future. The dramatic person continually faces the future where intentions become reality and dramatic events are enhanced.

Actors ought to realize that the past has an effect on the future. Psychologists diagnose some acute past experiences as traumatic if they are the cause of current symptoms, even if the original experience is not consciously remembered. Actors exploring the subtleties of their characters are urged to fabricate the past life and experiences of their characters. But they cannot stay there. Dramatists ought to use cybernetic thinking in order to speculate about the future behavior of their character. A psychological example is worth noting:

- *Traumatic experience occurs in childhood:* a barking dog attacks a little boy.
- *Adult symptom is noticed* when adult man jerks violently after a dog crosses his path.
- *The man does not think*, "That dog reminds me of the one I saw when I was a child."
- *The man's immediate thought is*, "That dog is going to attack me."
- *Instead of thinking of past*, the man projects what might happen in the future.[13]

So, too, actors might imagine traumatic symptoms in the past of their characters. However, if the script does not accentuate these symptoms, then the actor has to leave the fabrication and move into the present in order to play the character with integrity.

This discussion of past and future forms the foundation for exploring the relationship between drama and apocalyptic imagination. Like the actor, the preachers and teachers of apocalyptic literature are also required to be cybernetic thinkers, looking toward that complex and unknown future while being deeply rooted in the single line of the present. We always use the biblical tradition to ask necessary questions about the future, moving the community of faith to hope for that future.

In the next chapter, preachers and teachers encounter a model from tragic theatre that can be adapted to a more thorough understanding of apocalyptic literature. They will be able to use the model in order to sense where the congregation is at a certain time of crisis. Then, they can adapt their sermons and lectures to fit the space in which the congregation resides.

It helps, now and then, to step back
and take the long view.
The kingdom is not only beyond our efforts,
it is beyond our vision.
                    —*Attributed to Oscar Romero*[1]

Chapter Five

DRAMATIC CRISIS AND APOCALYPTIC LITERATURE

Not long ago, exercisers at St. Louis University Recreation Center could view four live, but muted, television monitors. One set pictured at least five shootings, a second showed the struggle of modern politics, a third depicted the lure of winning $1 million, and a fourth flaunted the human body as entertainment. These scenes coupled with thoughts generated by reading apocalyptic literature made me wonder if television ever gives hope. Is it possible that the superficial reality of television succeeds in masking a hope-filled world? Do we who preach and teach, also affected by television, reach community members who might feel as though they live in a world saturated with evil? How can we offer words of hope that might revivify the downtrodden and transform negative media images that might wash out societal hope?

Imaginative apocalyptic teachers and preachers need to ask questions like these from the point-of-view of those in crisis. Over and over again, the biblical authors of apocalyptic literature in both the First and Second Testaments asked questions for the people in real crises: a city in ruins, a temple once glorious but no longer so, a crisis of faith from an apathetic people, an abandoned tradition, the lures of a Greek world, inhumane suffering, the time the end will come, how to live it until that time, and concluding with the grand picture of the conflict between good and evil in the Book of Revelation. Then these authors reflected with the people about the God who would ultimately be victorious over all evil. Asking questions about crises is important, so it would be helpful to have a model that demonstrates how crisis literature works.

In Figure 2, I offer you a modified version of Richard Schechner's social crisis paradigm.[2] This figure is relevant for those experiencing crisis as well as those preparing to deal with crises, which is a reality for every human being in the unpredictable events of life. On a broader scale, the figure is also meant to critique social systems that are unique and subject to development. Profound justice questions stew within each person individually and among the community collectively, so preachers and teachers are required to address these questions. Working with apocalyptic literature can be a motivator for taking that transforming step.

Figure 2 describes the relationship between crisis in people's social lives and the dramatic experience that expresses a given social reality. With the assistance of the media, a social crisis (1), with the hidden social infrastructures that cause the crisis, is made public to the people affected by it (2). After becoming aware, attentive and creative persons (politicians, scientists, poets, and such) transform the social crisis into a dramatic experience (3). Catherine Keller remarks that performance of any apocalyptic script is not restricted to theatrical entertainment but also literalizes itself in history with the self-interpretation of dissident or reactionary actors on the scene of crisis. She rightly notes that crisis is routinely available to the true believer, who may interpret any crisis in such a way as to radically up the apocalyptic stake. For example, within the U.S. government, much apocalyptic religiosity showed forth the Book of Revelation's influence on U.S. policy in the 1980s.[3]

This dramatic experience (3) will reflect the shape of the social crisis and, thus, move the audience, often through its most vocal members, to seek integration (4) of the social crisis, helping them find a solution (5). The participants hope and dream for a new

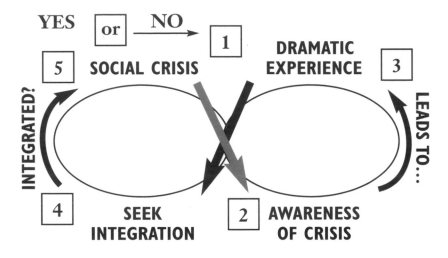

Figure 2. Dramatic Movement of Social Crisis

future (5), which resolves to assist in changing the value system that first caused the crisis. If the probable solution does not lead to integration given the social circumstances that have developed, the social crisis will issue forth in a new crisis (1), which then seeks resolution by repetition of the process. Nevertheless, this first effort has not been lost, because the action and interaction within this experience will usually be incorporated into subsequent dramatic experiences.

Victor Turner, who has recognized a similar four-step process of resolving a crisis, confirms the process described with Schechner's modified diagram. His language varies from what is already described: the breach, the crisis, the redress, and either reintegration or recognition of schism.

Because rituals are accompanied by transitions from one situation to another and from one cosmic or social world to another, this pattern can be employed in three ways in connection with preaching and teaching of apocalyptic literature. First, apocalyptic literature itself develops in this manner. A social crisis occurs in the society and gestates within the apocalyptic writer, who wishes to alert the community of the crisis along with its hidden social infrastructure. Thus, he or she writes a text that is dramatically imagined and taught or preached within an ancient worship experience or another dramatic experience. Perhaps the shape of the social crisis is made known so that integration may be achieved. If not, that same social crisis is again tackled after the apocalyptic writer has a new realization to present to the people.

Second, apocalyptic preachers and teachers can use this same paradigm. They study the background of the ancient apocalyptic text in order to understand its social crisis. Preachers and teachers then alert their audiences that the text's social crisis aligns with a current social catastrophe, along with the hidden infrastructure of that calamity. The imaginative preacher or teacher asks ,"In light of this text, what might be done to resolve the current crisis?" If the utilized word, coupled with the entire experience, has sparked the audience, then its members will emerge with a way for the community to assist in alleviating the calamity or even bring it to a conclusion.[4] However, if the community is not moved to seek integration, preachers/teachers know that they need to try again to move people's awareness and attention about the crisis by teaching another apocalyptic text, which might offer a different angle.[5] One hopes that a second attempt might awaken the assembly's imaginative integration of the crisis and lead to action and resolution. Turner confirms that religion as art continues to live as it is being performed only if its rituals are going concerns.

Table 2 shows the crisis model using the apocalyptic text from Daniel. Note how the flow is the same as that described in Figure 2. This important realization helps preachers and teachers experience apocalyptic texts as texts of crisis, which they sermonize or teach by correlation with a contemporary crisis.

Before moving forward to the third application involving the worshiping community, an excursion back to drama will illustrate the worship experience itself. Actor Mark Olsen, concerned with the spiritual dimension of acting, suggests a theatrical exercise. Go to the theatre and, during the performance, pull your awareness away from the stage and ask quietly, "What is going on here?"[6] This will direct your attention to the faces around you and draw you into the collective energy present. Simultaneously, the group of actors on stage is allowing their collective energy to descend upon the audience. That may lead you to ask for a second

Table 2. Crisis Categories Using the Book of Daniel

- **A social crisis occurs in society.**

  Even though the apocalyptic section of Daniel (7–12) indicates a time during the Babylonian captivity, it reflects the Maccabean revolt against the Romans. At that time, Daniel was concerned about the number of Jews embracing Hellenism and moving away from their tradition.

- **Crisis germinates within apocalyptic writer, who alerts his people.**

  Daniel's visions are addressed to the Jewish people, helping them see that there is a crisis with which they must deal in order to remain faithful to God.

- **Author uses dramatic imagination to write his visions.**

  Daniel 7–12 is a dramatic experience of visions, where Daniel uses his authority to convey his message to the people: Don't get caught up in Hellenism so that you lose your Jewish traditions. It doesn't matter here if Daniel is an actual person. The matter of concern is how the words affect the Jewish people.

- **The reading and preaching with dramatic imagination makes known the social crisis so that some understanding is achieved.**

  The words of Daniel are disseminated among the people, and some realize that their actions are turning them away from God and that the attack of the enemy is their punishment.

- **The reading and preaching with dramatic imagination does not achieve its purpose and so the process begins again with another vision and a different expression of the crisis or another crisis.**

  Daniel continues to have visions because more people need to be called back to their Jewish heritage. Perhaps another vision will help.

Note: The categories remain the same, but the way of alerting might change in order that the preacher, the teacher, and the listening community will come to an awareness of the modern crisis.

time, "What is going on here?" Olsen answers that there is transference of energy between stage and audience.[7]

The question, "What is going on here?" is the same question
the preacher or teacher of apocalyptic literature asks about the
audience. If there is collective energy between preachers/teachers
and the entire community, it has been fostered by the message,
the songs, the prayers and actions of the entire service or class.
That transferred energy will guide the community and encourage
action in response to the crisis. Preachers and teachers ought to
take seriously this energy transference. With its images of terror,
hope, and a cosmic viewpoint, teaching and preaching apocalyptic literature calls for an imaginative energy to be transferred from
ministers to the community. If members in the assembly do not
feel this imaginative energy, the process cannot proceed.

Now, return to Figure 2 and reflect upon the third way it may
be utilized for preaching and teaching apocalyptic literature.
Church members come to worship or students come to class with
valid expectations and potential energy. Preachers and teachers
cannot abdicate their responsibility to respond to and build upon
that energy. During the course of their preaching or lecture, they
ought to be in sync with the community's energy if they are to
credibly transfer imaginative energy. The audience is responsible
for developing their imagination by listening carefully to the
apocalyptic teacher or preacher and then carrying the spark created through the entire service with an intentional awareness.
Members envision the preached or spoken word within their
hearts and then pray during the service that they will unmask the
shape of the social infrastructure causing the crisis. Ministers who
creatively stage the worship service or the class will assist the
assembly to seek integration of the crisis. The entire event either
moves specific audience participants to integrate the crisis in their
minds and hearts or it doesn't. Thus, the worship or class experience may lead to action that might or might not assist in resolving that crisis. The result is movement to step 5 or back to step 1.

Viewing apocalyptic literature as drama is a way of stimulating
the imaginations of teacher, preacher, and listener. To be successful, the preacher and teacher need to work diligently to verbally
paint vibrant images from the apocalyptic text. Problems arise if

preachers or teachers have a *word* approach, which may have little impact beyond the listener's ear. However, we who preach or teach using an image approach may become skilled at developing potent images that will authorize audience members to creatively visualize a consequence or an action. Marva Dawn promotes an *image* approach by suggesting that we "paint the image with words [so that] everyone can imagine in their own way."[8] Chapters 6 and 7's exposition of First Testament apocalyptic texts and chapters 8 through 10's explanation of Second Testament apocalyptic texts offer exegetical examples to expand the teacher's and preacher's imagination for interpreting apocalyptic lectionary texts. The place of these apocalyptic texts in the various lectionaries is noted on the table in the Appendix.

The crisis diagram also indicates the vital relationship between drama and everyday life. The worshiping or studying community provides sociocultural frameworks of understanding and acting for other groups in which its members might be engaged. Victor Turner emphasizes this reality when he reminds actors that acting within everyday life is not merely reacting to analytical stimuli, but acts in frames that have been wrestled from the genres of cultural performances.

One could say worshiping, imagining, and acting are similar. Worshiping (imagining, acting) in everyday life is structured in such a way that one can identify with the modeling of those who presented the worship service (imagined, acted on stage). As a result, participants in the assembly (audience or classroom) move homeward in a reflective mood, asking how that minister, worship, class, or preaching (performance) changed their lives. Indeed, this worship experience (play) has moved the crisis into ordinary people's lives, where personal and group decisions are made to help avert continuation of the crisis. This is exactly what the apocalyptic preacher/imaginer wants to happen from the worship experience or the class.

As we move away from Schechner's crisis model, the essential truth to remember is that the worship service (the class or the stage) in its dramatic entirety is a priceless exegetical tool for preachers and teachers. Jana Childers affirms this by reminding us that performance is an avenue to develop creative imagination, which is so needed in teaching and preaching apocalyptic texts.

When the sermon and the entire worship service or the lecture is understood as performance in a theatre, then principles of theatre become a path upon which preachers and teachers may walk. In *Performing the Word: Preaching as Theatre*, Jana Childers offers a convincing argument that preaching and theatre need to be elevated to the highest esteem possible in order to enhance all disciplines. She proposes a trip to the often-unexplored country of the imagination, where all people may enjoy equality. On that trip, these people may discover muscles never used as well as a comfortable supply of oxygen that gives new energy to their efforts. In other words, they develop a common worldview.[9]

The key to a common worldview for drama, teaching, and preaching of apocalyptic literature is how one thinks of art. For some, art may be only decorative. For others, art is alive among those whose hearts and heads are open to ecstasy. Childers captures this fascination by noting that theatre delights in vagueness, concurrence, and tensiveness.

If a lively sermon or lecture is created, hearers may be led to experience the Holy Spirit swirling in the heartbeat of the faith community. Poet Amos Wilder describes that swirling of Spirit as an adventure that might take its hearers to places they would rather not go:

> Draw near to the holy mountain,
>   as to Sinai enveloped in smoke
>   with its tremor and flowing lava.
> To draw near is to
>   take your life in your hand.
> Going to church [being in a faith community] is like
>   approaching an open volcano,
>   where the world is molten
>   and hearts are sifted.[10]

This is a way to think about what we are creating within a worship service or an apocalyptic teaching. God, par excellence, urges people to draw near the volcanic ash of the earth upon which they live and allow it to constantly change its molten forms so that evil will be buried in the lava flow. Thus, using the preacher or teacher as intermediary, God moves faithful hearts toward the Messiah who reveals God's truth in the drama of salvation. Christian apocalyptic texts describe Jesus as that promised Messiah, but still call listeners to openness to that Spirit of Jesus living among us. The drama of salvation is played out in every era of history.

An active homiletic for apocalyptic literature elevates preaching and teaching to an event of the community rather than being only words spoken. Preaching and teaching are processes that move images from the biblical text to transform people hungering for God's face and voice. Scripture notes that only certain people see God or hear God's voice (see Exod 33:11, 20, 23, and 34:29–35). The preacher's and teacher's task is to be open in prayer to the sight and voice of God so that God's word may be voiced with imagination.

This mirrors drama, for it, too, is a process of moving words, gestures, and directions from a script through actors to theatergoers who come with hunger for meaning. These theatergoers sit on the edge of their seats waiting for the curtain to rise and a spark of energy to burst forth. Talented actors perform scenes that enable watchers and hearers to visualize the action of God's Spirit alive in the drama's ambiance.

While these artistic events of preaching/teaching apocalyptic and acting share common ground, nevertheless, they are not equivalent. Frustrated parishioners exit from the liturgy saying, "I wish our preacher wouldn't be so dramatic," and theatergoers exit at intermission with frustration, saying, "There's just too much moralizing in this play." Both reactions are usually spoken with discouragement.

However, some are exhilarated with the preaching and teaching of apocalyptic and/or with the dramatic event. They have embraced the Spirit whirling within the community and have caught the truth offered. These churchgoers (class members or theatergoers) allow art to be more than a decoration—to be that transforming Spirit of energy bringing new life within the community. And if, perchance, a hand reaches to the other side of the aisle, two persons might find some perceptions that will lead to common ground.

The imagined sharing that takes place might assist the reader in seeing how the Spirit can be at work in a community's dramatic worship. James Young's invitation into the realm of art might also apply to dramatic worship, preaching, and teaching:

- Art is not about lessons, but illumination.
- Art is not about persuasion, but epiphanies.
- Art is not about decision, but discovery.
- Art does not aim at entertainment, but pleasure.
- Art uncovers ambiguities in hope of pointing to truth.[11]

Substituting "preaching/teaching of apocalyptic literature" for "art" in the preceding statements gives clarity to the image making attempted by the preacher/teacher:

- Preaching/teaching of apocalyptic literature is not about lessons, but illumination.
- Preaching/teaching of apocalyptic literature is not about persuasion, but epiphanies.
- Preaching/teaching of apocalyptic literature is not about decision, but discovery.
- Preaching/teaching apocalyptic literature does not aim at entertainment, but pleasure. ("Pleasure" for preaching/teaching apocalyptic literature comes when we give people hope that God will, in the end, win over all evil. This frees them to praise God.)
- Preaching/teaching of apocalyptic literature uncovers ambiguities in hope of pointing to truth.

Note that both preaching/teaching of apocalyptic literature and art can be learned in lessons, can be persuasive, can be entertaining (if you read apocalyptic literature with imagination), can be helpful for decision making and can uncover ambiguities. Thus, these statements reflect a *both/and* perspective of acting in relation to preaching and teaching rather than an *either/or* perspective.

The comparisons in this chapter have established the necessity of paralleling drama and preaching/teaching of apocalyptic literature. Both require imaginative words as well as words of experience. Both the preacher and teacher who interpret texts and the actor who interprets a character can rely on their experiences to take words out of the scriptures (scripts) and fill them with the spirit of the message. The spirit that motivates these professions requires an honest preaching/teaching (performance), one that emanates from internal integrity. While using imaginative expressions, preachers/teachers of apocalyptic literature (actors) must discover honesty and truthfulness. They do their work without deceit, making themselves present in their words and actions. These honest, disciplined preachers/teachers (actors) speak a word of truth with a feeble heart and are altered spiritually from within as they exhort congregations or classes (audiences) to become truthful, disciplined, and honest. To that spirituality of preaching and teaching apocalyptic and of acting we now turn.

PARALLEL SPIRITUAL RENEWAL OF ACTORS AND APOCALYPTIC PREACHERS

Mark Olsen is convinced that there is a spirituality for actors. He describes how he grew up thinking that if he was nice to people, if he obeyed the commandments and did good deeds in his life, then he would surely enter heaven upon his death. As a teenager, it was popular in his circle of friends to scoff at the notion of death. Later in life, however, he had a number of extraordinary experiences that compelled him to become educated in spiritual matters. Distancing himself from both consensus and rebellion, Olsen saw the desperation in the faces of adults who seemed to be running, trying to escape something or someone.

Nothing is as it seems, Olsen concluded. He realized that, if he stepped into the world of spiritual advancement, he was entering through a looking glass into realms where the rational mind has no footing. Olsen concluded that the spiritual journey is not easy, for it is all about transformation, and most people do not realize the amount of work needed to transform. After becoming involved in acting, Olsen knew that his spiritual awakening would touch other actors if he could convince them to embrace such a transformative process. He was never sure that others would be interested. However, moving forward as if they were, Olsen succeeded in drawing a few seekers into the spiritual journey each time he shared his own spiritual awakening.

What Olsen discovered is that those who performed night after night, day after day, were as hungry for depth in their lives as he had once been. Each day actors ready themselves to put on an act or to *act with the inspiration of God*. Olsen is convinced that, if the latter happens, great stage acting will emanate from their deepest human understandings. Olsen suggests that this quest for a deeper, more intimate understanding of humanity is the spiritual dimension of acting.[12]

What actors discover by working with Olsen is akin to what students of teaching and preaching discover from the beginning of their learning experience. They cannot step into the classroom or the pulpit with the integrity needed to teach or preach the gospel unless they have developed a personal spirituality, one that fervently desires to feed God's hungry people. If they work at it, these students will become aware of the change happening within them as they seek God's Spirit, change that assists them to embody the authentic word of God for others.

Asking questions about the spiritual process stimulates growth. If students or congregations settle for an answer too quickly, they risk missing the process of growth necessary for an imaginative teaching or preaching ministry. They forge ahead in the journey by delving deeper and deeper. As they travel the road, they develop an imaginative heart.

As Olsen discovered with performers, this process cannot be imposed. So, too, with preachers and teachers, who must seek out a more vibrant spirituality and not wait for it to come to them. Table 3 clarifies the performer process recommended by Olsen that is analogous to the spiritual journey of apocalyptic preachers and teachers. Those in the community might also be interested in the spiritual journey, and preachers and teachers need to encourage such desire. They ought to communicate the importance of the members' own spiritual renewal, which will lead them to full participation in the liturgical service or class work.

For performers who embrace the journey, Olsen offers these cautionary words:

- It takes courage and fortitude to awaken.
- A great deal of energy is needed to sustain one through the trials and tribulations of the path.
- Sacrifices must be made.
- The idea of success cannot dominate your energy.
- A new flow of God's energy assists one to be patient and enduring with the realization that there are unlimited resources from God.

Table 3. The Journey of Spiritual Renewal for Performer and Preacher/Teacher

For Performers	For Apocalyptic Preacher/Teacher
The performer surrenders to the character, with no craving for reward.	The apocalyptic preacher/teacher surrenders to the Spirit of God with no craving for reward, but God gives the gift of imagination.
Performers are encouraged to recognize the gifts that exist in their choice of profession.	An apocalyptic preacher/teacher recognizes that gifts abound with their choice of preaching God's word—most important, a relationship with God through prayer
The performer pays a debt to the universe by working toward unification.	The apocalyptic teacher/preacher pays a debt to the universe by aiding in the work of giving hope amid crisis.
This process is the higher purpose a performer must achieve in order to be attuned with audience desires.	This process is the higher purpose that an apocalyptic teacher/preacher must achieve in order to be attuned to congregational needs in crisis times.

Performers are taught that each person may have a different higher purpose—so a performer's higher purpose may not match anyone else's.	Apocalyptic preachers/teachers are cautioned that each person's spiritual journey is individual, so they might not be able to enter into this time of crisis.
This could be a frightening experience for the performer, but it need not be, for the spirit of their profession is grace and peace.	Facing crises may be frightening for the apocalyptic preacher/teacher, but the promise of experiencing God's hope and possibility may overcome any fear that occurs.
The personal work of the performer may not challenge the audience, but a good performance can impel growth in the values of the audience.	The apocalyptic teacher/preacher has a direct opportunity to challenge the community so that they aren't just showing up to be fed, but are real participants in the community and world crises.

- One must sacrifice a fixed self-image. The courage to always be a learner, to risk looking foolish while giving up the need to be treated as special are all a part of this spiritual journey.
- Last, seek out authentic spiritual guidance. One's perceptions and readiness will lead one to the guide most suitable for their particular stage of development.[13]

All of this strongly resonates with the bona fide journey of the teacher and preacher of apocalyptic as well as the authentic spiritual journey of each believer. The performing arts could be shallow without teachers like Olsen willing to display their convictions that deepen the experience of those seeking friendship with the divine. Focusing on the apocalyptic dream, that time when all evil will be destroyed, requires a spirituality of conviction that moves one to continue wading in the waters that rise as one seeks God (see Ezek 47:1–12).

In those times, the spiritual life of the apocalyptic preacher or teacher needs the same kind of encouragement that Olsen provides for actors—he challenges them, especially new actors, to join with the ancient actor and make even the smallest, most insipid assignment a spiritual task. He concludes that this is the secret of overcoming the powerful current of mediocrity now being faced within the theatrical world.

The spiritual journey of the teacher and preacher must be challenged just as rigorously. Preachers and teachers of apocalyptic literature must be willing to wait upon the Spirit in disciplined prayer so that they are able to reach out effectively to an unsettled, waiting world in crisis.

Even though the official biblical canon was closed centuries ago, the Spirit is capable of opening new insights for the receptive and pliable hearts of those who preach or teach apocalyptic literature. Indeed, the ancient text joins the preacher or teacher of apocalyptic to the ancient writers who embraced the future by living in the present time of crisis. These apocalyptic writers probably made the smallest, most insipid task an essential part of the spiritual journey. They overcame the powerful current of evil turned into crisis for the people of the covenant. Through a dramatic text, these apocalyptic writers gave God's people hope, persuading them that evil would never have the final answer. Apocalyptic preachers and teachers in today's crises must learn to model the spirituality of the apocalyptic writers to give the people of God in our day the same hope and vision.

CONCLUSION

Preachers and teachers of apocalyptic literature must be able to stand within their community as those among many who are oriented to live the peace-and-justice challenge of God's word. They must not lose the urgent sense of awe and responsibility that comes with the daunting task of preaching or teaching the word of God during crisis. Martin Marty reminds teachers and preachers that their prayer life is crucial to this task. He notes that prayer is a greatly underutilized form in connection with creativity.[14] Human creativity can only be involved in divine creativity if faithfulness to prayer leads preachers and teachers of apocalyptic literature to an encounter with that divine creativity. Teaching and preaching apocalyptic literature creates saving grace in the community now, as it becomes a means of God's dynamic self-disclosure.

Since the terrorist attacks of September 11, 2001, have muddied their lives, U.S. citizens have been in need of saving grace. All who are in crisis now need these graces as urgently as those who received the apocalyptic word centuries before. Some have sought this grace in faith, but others have wavered in the face of devastating economic crisis. The apocalyptic writer's message was clearly for communities in crisis, usually as a result of greed by those who unjustly dominated. In this chapter, Schechner's model, adapted in Figure 2, has been used to facilitate the learning of teachers and preachers so that they analyze and connect their current crises with those of the apocalyptic writer. It is only in that way that preachers and teachers of apocalyptic literature will discover the virtue of saving hope, even in their own despair, in order to preach and teach the drama of salvation as boldly and effectively as apocalyptic writers in centuries past to their communities in crisis.

In the next five chapters, we look at the various texts of apocalyptic literature present in the current canon of our Bibles. Four texts are from the First Testament, while the others are given to us in the Second Testament. It is my hope that this material will assist both teachers and preachers as they encounter this perplexing material, perhaps for the first time. I am also hopeful that this *staging* of biblical texts will teach both teachers and preachers that they need not shy away from this very hopeful literature.

We accomplish in our lifetime only a fraction of
the magnificent enterprise that is God's work.
Nothing we do is complete,
which is another way of saying
that the kingdom always lies beyond us.
            —*Attributed to Oscar Romero*[1]

Chapter Six

UNMASKING APOCALYPTIC LITERATURE: ISAIAH, EZEKIEL

Among the human experiences people share, the most agonizing is undoubtedly the experience of death. When a loved one dies, a person might feel that the world is at an end. In order to cope—that is, to have hope—they either hide their grief for a future time or engage in a process of healing, calling upon God for strength. That very act of calling upon God is an act of hope, for persons experiencing the death of a loved one realize that they cannot face the future alone. In hope, they allow the Spirit to lift them out of death and into new life.

Edward Hirsch shares a poignant example of Polish poets being lifted out of death. He writes that the poets who survived World War II were "initiated in the apocalyptic fires of history."[2] The spirit of their work was shaped by their collective experience of disaster. The poet Czeslaw Milosz was optimistic, growing up during one of the few periods of Polish independence, but he became extremely pessimistic after the war. Seeking freedom from the dead, Milosz wrote a poem called "Dedication" ending in utter despair.

They used to pour millet on graves or poppy seeds
To feed the dead who would come disguised as birds.
I put this book here for you, who once lived
So that you should visit us no more.[3]

Younger Polish poets, a new generation, were drawn into this trauma without experiencing it. They observed war-surviving poets who wrote as if they could never believe in the future again. These new poets questioned the poetic shift from optimism to pessimism and wondered how that shift contributed to the aesthetic values within their society. These poets emerged with a new kind of poetry, reinvented from the ground up. Their poems were simple and naked, yet life giving and hopeful. Tadeusz Rozewicz caught this spirit of dire simplicity in his poem "In the Midst of Life":

After the end of the world
after death.
    I found myself in the midst of life
    creating myself
    building life
    people animals landscape.[4]

These youthful poets attempted to tell the truth about agonizing suffering, but they refused to despair. They expressed with hope the possibility of living meaningful lives after that suffering.

Involved in crisis situations, the apocalyptic writers of the First Testament experienced this same spirit, driving the community from void into fullness, from despair into hope. This experience of despair to hope is the strength of the First Testament apocalyptic passages, which are highlighted in the next two chapters. I examine portions of three prophetic texts that have been identified as apocalyptic: Isaiah 24–27, Ezekiel 1–3 and 38–39, and Zechariah 9–14. I also investigate Daniel 7–12, which has always been recognized as apocalyptic. Each text will be examined with three important steps:

1. The historical situation of the text
2. The words of hope from that writer

3. Practical suggestions for preaching and teaching the apocalyptic text in a dramatic way

UNMASKING APOCALYPTIC ISAIAH

Apocalyptic qualities have long been found in Isaiah 24–27, where Isaiah speaks to the remnant about the devastation of the world. Referring back to the definition in chapter 1 (p. 11), some of these apocalyptic qualities are as follows:

- Isaiah experiences a vision: "See, the Lord is going to…" (24:1).
- He lives in a period of crisis: "The ruined city lies desolate…" (24:10).
- Isaiah's call included Seraphim, who delivered the live coal to his lips (6:6–7).
- The desolation is relativized by the elders on Mount Zion who glorify God reigning in Jerusalem (24:23–25:1).
- The eschatological event in question will neither be hastened nor thwarted by human efforts, but will unfold, true to an eternal plan. The fourfold use of "on that day" within these three chapters emphasizes that God is the executor, not humans.

Isaiah 24–27 juxtaposes two cities: a city of chaos, symbol of godlessness, and the city of God's people, a symbol of Jerusalem. Ancient commentators were persuaded to identify Isaiah 24–27 as an entirely distinct section in the Book of Isaiah. In a 1938 commentary, Johannes Lindbloom called these chapters a visionary cantata composed at the time of the fall of Babylon.[5] Because of the earlier work of many scholars, there is now general agreement that Isaiah 24–27 was one of the latest sections added by the final editor. A postexilic date is likely.

Isaiah's Community in Crisis

By 587 BCE, the Babylonians had sent all the influential people to exile in Babylon, a city that lies on the left bank of the Euphrates, not far south of the modern Baghdad. This period, filled with crisis, resulted in losses of land and kingship. Prophetic writers of that time gave voice to some people's frustrations with foreign rule and their cry to an invisible God who may have even abandoned them. These people listened to the prophetic voices for clues as to whether God would still be with them and how they would finally return to their beloved city Jerusalem. Until that time, they were told to get on with their lives in Babylon instead of continuing to mourn their losses (see Jer 29:1ff). God would set the time for their return.

Isaiah affirms that God has not abandoned them. When that day comes (approximately 532 BCE), it will be an occasion for great rejoicing: "They shout from the west over the majesty of the Lord; in the east [they] give glory to the Lord" (24:14b–15a).

Isaiah's Words of Hope

By treating Isaiah 24–27 as a distinct reality, it is possible to recognize images of hope in the midst of terror. The first striking quality of Isaiah 24–27 is its poetic style and its complex images, which invite one's mind to dance, even in the midst of disaster. God shines through the text, offering hope to a people in crisis. Chapter 24 is studied in three subsections: 24:1–13, 24:14–20, and 24:21–23.

Isaiah 24:1–13 is a universal view of the world's devastation. Written in the first person, it emphasizes the city of chaos, a symbol of godlessness, for the time cries out with urgency. An alternate translation uses "city of nothingness" *(NJB)*, which might express a more devastating city. Chaos keeps people thinking that there is still something left in Jerusalem; nothingness refers to a completely naked city.

The vocabulary of Isaiah 24 is reminiscent of that used for the destruction of Nineveh by the prophet Nahum (2:11), who speaks in anger about the cities that have plundered Jerusalem and writes in irony of the destruction of that same city. Grief and lament are juxtaposed against the withering of vegetation. "The wine dies up, the vine languishes" (24:7a) is coupled with "It is within the land, among the people, as with an olive tree after it is beaten" (24:13ab).

Isaiah 24:14–20 contrasts two attitudes, the cheerful voices of those saved and the woeful voices of those who fear that the city's destruction is not enough. The Hebrew of Isaiah 24:16a includes a problematic word that could mean "glory" or "beauty," which leads to two different translations: "glory to the Righteous One" or "beauty to the righteous nation." If the translation is "glory," then the phrase refers to God, whose name was not said aloud in Judaism.[6] If the word means "beauty," then it could refer either to God or to the righteous in general who exult at the destruction of all wickedness. In both cases, there is cause for hope.

Finally, Isaiah 24:21–23 clarifies that God has destroyed the city of godlessness and now reigns on Mount Zion in Jerusalem, glorious in the sight of all who are not in wickedness. This might seem like an angry God, but the reader must remember that Jewish writers penned these texts. Their perspective is that God is caring for the Jewish people and is faithful to them, no matter what happens to others. Battles happen between people; God does not instigate a battle. No matter what the situation, the text proclaims that all creation now reflects apocalyptic hope.

Isaiah 25 begins with the "castle of the insolent," no longer a place for foreigners, which suggests that God has freed the covenant people. This is an extremely hopeful chapter, as God is "a refuge to the poor, a refuge to the needy in their distress" (25:4a) and also one who will "wipe away the tears from all faces" (25:8a). The Lord of Hosts, proclaimed king on Mount Zion (24:23b), now invites all God's people to a coronation meal. Isaiah 25:10–12a interrupts the celebration, mentioning specifically that Moab will be "trodden down as straw is trampled down in manure" (*NIV* Interlinear). Used paradoxically, this verse emphasizes a situation that the people cannot accomplish unless they completely rely upon God. The apocalyptic writer wishes to squelch the human pride that remains hidden within God's covenant people, a pride that would tend to move them away from hope.

Isaiah 26 proclaims a hopeful hymn to the city of Zion and contrasts it with the strong city that God has humiliated (Isa 26:5–6). A wisdom teaching in 26:7–11 uplifts the good people, even though they experienced humiliation. Isaiah 26:12–13 returns to the song of thanksgiving. God wishes *shalom* to a people who have repented from their evil deeds, a sign of hope for all who open themselves to the unique touch of God.

An interesting aside about wishing *shalom* comes from a Jewish rabbi, who told me that the biblical meaning is an expression that all the pieces of one's life might be integrated. If we Christians practiced this meaning of *shalom*, our peace greetings would "bind up the brokenhearted,...proclaim liberty to the captives and release to the prisoners...to comfort all who mourn; to provide for those who mourn in Zion" (Isa 61:1b, 2c–3a, proclaimed by Jesus [Luke 4:18]). This greeting of *shalom* would wish ardent hope to that person.

Referring back to the text being studied, a song of lament compared to a woman's experience of labor follows (26:15–18). This is a text of anxiety, because the enlargement of the nation has not brought salvation to the earth nor given birth to people in the world (Isa 26:18b). Verse 26:14 assures the reader that the dead enemies will never again inhabit the land. However, the people ought to hope that those Jews who died will again come to life and fill the land (26:19). Chapter 26 concludes by warning the just that they are to hide in their private rooms so that, when God returns to crush the enemies (26:21), the faithful will not be harmed.

Chapter 27 exaggerates the earlier themes. Allusions to the evil in the city are now magnified with the mention of "Leviathan, the twisting serpent" (27:1c). In ancient mythology, the monsters from the sea represent the most dangerous enemies, for they cannot be defeated by human strength but only by one mightier. Therefore, God slays the monster of the sea. God's conquest encourages the faithful to "sing about a fruitful vineyard," which God has promised to watch over (27:2–3). Israel will again blossom and bear fruit and the shalom they speak to a triumphant God will plant them firmly in God's house.

Isaiah 27:7–11 describes Jacob, whose guilt is atoned by the destruction of the enemy. As Jacob is used here, it is symbolic for God's people. Thus, the text is saying that all the sins of the people have been atoned. However, the text's images are dry and lifeless because the guilt upon the people is heavy. "The fortified city is solitary, a habitation deserted and forsaken, like the wilderness" (27:10a).

Nevertheless, there is the hopeful regathering in the city where a great trumpet blows, calling all people to "worship the Lord on the holy mountain of Jerusalem" (27:13b), the mountain of all hope. Imagine the trumpet as the *shofar*, a ram's horn blown by the ancient Hebrews during religious ceremonies and also as a signal in battle. The *shofar* is still used in the synagogue during Rosh Hashanah, the Jewish New Year (celebrated on the first and second days of *Tishri*, our September–October) and at the end of Yom Kippur, a day marked by fasting and prayer for atonement of sins (the tenth day of *Tishri*). While using the *shofar*, the Jewish people today recall that same hopefulness, as if they are on that same holy mountain in Jerusalem.

Preaching and Teaching Hope from Apocalyptic Isaiah

I want to remind preachers of one basic rule in preparation of a sermon: the muscle of the sermon is contained in its structure, not in its ornaments. The same would be true in preparing to teach a class. In order to assist preachers and teachers who encounter an apocalyptic passage of Isaiah in the lectionary (see the Appendix), who are preparing to teach a class on Isaiah, or who choose to use Isaiah during a time of crisis, I suggest several focus statements along with their accompanying function statements.[7] I also include a basic outline of the structure that a sermon or class might take. Of course, this basic organizational plan is only the beginning of sermons and lectures. These must be personalized using stories from the preacher's or teacher's own experience and the experience of the community.

Plan A

Focus: Even though evil is all around us, God still comes to us with hope (Isa 24).

Function: To enable the hearers to retain hope in spite of the evils they see all around them

    I.   God presents a universal plan for the destruction of evil.

        A. God's holy people will lament and grieve.

      B. Nature mourns in the same way.

      C. The city of Jerusalem is no more.

  II. God detects differing attitudes among God's people.

      A. The saved cheer joyfully.

      B. Some cry woefully, fearing that God does not do enough.

      C. In either case, God assures the faithful that Mount Zion reigns gloriously.

  III. God speaks in our life experience.

      A. We, too, lament the presence of evil in our world.

      B. However, we can only do something about our own evil.

      C. We hope that God will assist us in finding a way out of all evils.

Plan B

Focus: God frees the covenant people (Isa 25).

Function: To enable hope-filled hearers to find God in freedom of response

  I. God frees the poor, the needy, and the depressed.

      A. God is a refuge for the poor and needy.

      B. God will wipe away all tears.

  II. God invites these hope-filled faithful to celebrate freedom at the coronation meal on Mount Zion.

      A. Those attending must still be purged of pride.

      B. Complete reliance on God brings one to freedom and hope.

  III. God continues to free us today as we walk the journey in hope.

      A. How do we rely on our own power instead of God's mercy?

      B. When and why do we need tears wiped away?

      C. How has Christ worked through us in reaching out to those who are more poor and needy than ourselves?

      D. The coronation meal on Mount Zion is our free gift for remaining hopeful.

Plan C

Focus: God's *shalom* invites all to wholeness/holiness on the journey in hope (Isa 26).

Function: To enable the hearers to be more compassionate as they reach out in *shalom* to the members of the world community

   I. God touches each person in a unique way.
     A. God lifts some from humiliation.
     B. God allows some to see their evil ways.
     C. God labors with some as a mother labors to give birth.

   II. A teaching about *shalom*.
     A. Biblical meaning: an integration of all the pieces of our life.
     B. God touches others through us.

   III. The meaning of our Christian *shalom*.
     A. How our attitudes can be blocks to true *shalom* during our liturgies and classroom teaching.
     B. How those attitudes must change if we are to give people hope with our expression of *shalom*.

Plan D

Focus: We remain hopeful because God atones for human sinfulness (Isa 27).

Function: To enable hope-filled hearers to experience the forgiveness of God

   I. God forgives Jacob.
     A. Why the biblical Jacob is symbolic of all people.
     B. How atonement leaves one dry and lifeless.
     C. Guilt is a heavy burden.

   II. God gathers the hope-filled faithful on Mount Zion.
     A. The *shofar* calls people to the mountain.
     B. How the Jews use the *shofar* today.

III. God's atonement in our own lives today.
   A. How we take our guilt to God: beginning of liturgy, sacrament of reconciliation, spiritual direction, companioning with another loved one.
   B. How and where we hear the blowing of the *shofar* in our lives.
   C. How our hope strengthens us to experience the atonement of God.

UNMASKING APOCALYPTIC EZEKIEL

The visionary life of the prophet Ezekiel is inspiring but often comical. A former colleague encouraged students to enlarge their imaginations as he nicknamed Ezekiel "everybody's favorite zany." Yes, students found humor in the comical ways Ezekiel preached and taught God's word, but these students repeatedly exclaimed how this prophet nurtured the hopeful thought that God would be with them. Chapters 1–3 and 38–39 are generally agreed to be the apocalyptic sections of the Book of Ezekiel. These five chapters are studied in several sections. Ezekiel 1–3 is taken as a whole, while Ezekiel 38–39 are considered individually.

Ezekiel is one of the most visually oriented of the Hebrew prophets. In the book's first verse, the prophet is invited to be privy to the intentions of the Holy One by means of visions. As a recipient of God's mysteries, Ezekiel is addressed throughout as "son of man."[8] In later Jewish and Christian settings, this unusual expression represents an apocalyptic figure associated with God's triumph at the end of time (see Dan 7:12–14). What was Ezekiel's community experiencing?

Ezekiel's Community in Crisis

Ezekiel's career as prophet began on the River Chebar among the first wave of exiles (597 BCE). He was called to communicate God's plan as they heard rumors about the impending destruction of Jerusalem. The tribe of Judah (the Southern Kingdom) had not heeded the warning of earlier prophets and thus was subject to the same treatment by the Babylonians as Israel (the Northern Kingdom) received from the Assyrians. At the time of the destruction of the Temple in Jerusalem, the second wave of exiles arrived in Babylon (587 BCE). Whether Ezekiel ever prophesied to these new exiles is not indicated in the text.

Nevertheless, crisis reigned for all these exiles. First, they were now living in a foreign land. Second, they had lost their monarchy. Third, these exiles wondered if they should establish roots in Babylon (see Jer 29:1ff). Finally, their Temple in Jerusalem was destroyed. Where was their God now? Why did God not use authority to save them?

It is important to note that, at this time in Jewish history, the people thought God dwelt in the Temple alone. So, if there was any threat upon the Temple, it would feel to the people that God had abandoned them. Since it had also been revealed to them that their God was dominant and could destroy the armies of Egypt (see Exod 3:7–9), it could be said that their faith was weak at this time. They could not understand why God had not intervened. They needed Ezekiel's assistance.

Ezekiel's Words of Hope

In the inaugural vision (Ezek 1), God lures the prophet Ezekiel by providing him with images he knew very well from his days in the Temple. However, God's throne is described in a uniquely symbolic way: God coming to the exiles on wheels (see 1:15–21). Such glory humbled Ezekiel (1:28c), but he soon realized that the vision was to be shared with the people. The vital power of God's Spirit uplifted Ezekiel and gave him a mission: "Mortal [son of man], I am sending you to the people of Israel" who have rebelled against me (2:3a). "Do not be afraid of their words…and do not be dismayed at their looks, for they are a rebellious house. You shall speak my words to them, whether they hear or refuse to hear" (2:6b, 7a).

Obeying God proved a daunting task for Ezekiel. First, he is given a scroll as sweet as honey in order to fortify him to go to the exiles (3:1–3). The frightened Ezekiel knew his history. The people would refuse to listen to him, for they have not even listened to God (2:3–8). Ezekiel "went in bitterness in the heat of [his] spirit" (3:14b), for he needed prodding to allow the Spirit to lift him up and take him to the people.

After arrival, Ezekiel sat among them for seven days, stunned.[9] God teaches Ezekiel that his hesitation costs, and he is struck dumb. Note that the literal meaning of the Hebrew is extremely graphic. God will make the tongue of Ezekiel stick to the roof of his mouth, so that he will be silent and unable to rebuke the people. A Second Testament comparison to Ezekiel's condition is Zechariah, who received a vision in the inner sanctuary and was struck dumb and deaf (see Luke 1:22). Because of his condition, Ezekiel is then told to go to his house (3:26). Only later, when God tells Ezekiel to speak, is he ready to embrace his mission as watchman. Ezekiel is to convey to the Israelites that God is with them.

There are at least three reasons for preachers and teachers to express hope from this apocalyptic text:

1. God used Ezekiel's human limitations as a tool to emphasize that God would lead him in hope. Preachers and teachers, too, need to allow God to use them and to lead them in hope.
2. Ezekiel's experience of the authenticity of the vision seemed bleak at first, but God changed Ezekiel's attitudes. The exiles were changed by Ezekiel's prophesying, and they looked forward to a full restoration, even while in captivity. Preachers' and teachers' attitudes ought to be changed by God at the same time that their preaching or class is trying to change others.
3. Ezekiel's ultimate experience of God allowed him to trust in God's sustaining concern. Preachers and teachers alike ought to be open to the experience of God as sustainer.

Chapters 38 and 39 are the heart of Ezekiel's apocalyptic material. In these chapters, Ezekiel is told to prophesy in the country of Magog against Gog, who is about to invade Israel from the north (38:2). Perhaps Magog was introduced here for the rhyme of names, but historically we know that Magog was often associated with Meshech and Tubal, cities on the south coast of the Black Sea. This vision must have predicted a future invasion, because Ezekiel is now prophesying to the people in exile. They have not yet returned to their land. Because of this time warp, some commentators think that the text might also represent the apocalyptic struggle between good and evil at the end time.

What is to be made of chapters 38–39 when they seem intrusive to the flow of events in the text? Chapters 33–37 are hopeful words promising everlasting possession of the land with a Davidic prince and an everlasting covenant. Chapters 40–48 follow 33–37 with a detailed description of the Temple and a description of the transition leading up to the restoration. Instead of a smooth transition from 37 to 40, chapters 38 to 39 imagine a future when Israel has returned to its land and is experiencing a mysterious invasion from a northern tribe.

Ezekiel 34:25–28 contains the key to understanding these chapters. Ezekiel had prophesied in God's name that the Israelites would "be secure on their soil…[and] no more be plunder for the nations" (34:27b, 28a). This passage contrasts with an earlier prophecy of Jeremiah about an invasion from a mysterious enemy who would throw them into chaos (Jer 4:23–26).

Many would have found the promise of chapter 34 unbelievable, for they had recently experienced the devastating collapse of Jerusalem (587 BCE). Ezekiel realizes that the people may not have recognized their own weakness at the time of the Babylonian invasion. They had not lived according to the covenant they had made with their God. Chapters 38 to 39 are significant, then, because they reassure the people that God is neither powerless nor neglectful of the covenant people. Ezekiel proposes that this attack, nor any other attack, need not be feared. These chapters spell out the confidence the Israelites should have in their God.

As chapter 38 begins, Ezekiel is told to "set his face against Gog" (38:2, *NIV* Interlinear) and announce the divine opposition to his army. The text reminds us of two important things: (1) that Israel is undefended, with no walls, no bars, and no gates, and (2) that the people are now dwelling securely under God's care (38:10–13). Ezekiel wonders if some are still complacent. Will Gog, an enemy greedy for possessions, overtake them?

The text denies this happenstance. God's control (38:3) leads to negative consequences for Gog. God is against this enemy, no matter at what indefinite time in the future this battle takes place. God is revealed as present and concerned, planning to attack anyone who invades "*my* people" (38:14).

The cosmic, apocalyptic perspective of Gog's attack begins with a great earthquake that rattles the land and terrifies the animals (38:18–23). This creates panic in the people. Will the warriors of Gog kill one another? No. Instead God brings a legal process against Gog that is filled with descriptions of plagues, hailstones, and fire (38:22). The community may have remembered the dreadful destruction of Sodom and Gomorrah (Gen 19:24–28). God's purpose is shown forth: "I will display my greatness and my holiness and make myself known in the eyes of many nations. Then they shall know that I am the Lord" (38:23).

The defeat of Gog by the Most High is announced in Ezekiel 39. Teachers and preachers might be inclined to think of this text as a vivid description of an actual battle, an eyewitness description. This is inaccurate, for the Bible is never a text that shows *how* God acts. Instead, it is an account by a writer who wishes to show *that* God acts for those who are faithful. Nevertheless, the text is extremely graphic: "I will turn you around, and I will lead you by the nose, and I will bring you up, and I will lead you in."[10] The choice of three strong verbs (*turn, lead,* and *bring*) forcefully describes the fall of Gog. The Israelites can be confidently assured that God has saved them (39:5b).

Notice how the language becomes progressively more passionate. The selection of words (see Ezek 39:8, 11, 14) seems almost ironic or sarcastic because Israel's own defenseless security had prompted Gog to launch this attack in the first place. God even uses the once-weak people in the destruction of massive armaments (39:9–10). God's holiness, with a plea to no longer profane this name, woos the people back to God.

Destruction of weapons and desolation of soldiers' bodies indicate the overwhelming defeat of Gog by Israel. God's justice shines forth as the nations see God's glory (39:21). However, it is not the end of the present order, for the reader is brought full circle to a time before the enemy attacked (39:25–29). The fortunes of Jacob are restored. God is merciful to the people, the only time this verb is used in all of Ezekiel. Thus, the Holy One who had once been hidden would never be so again (39:24, 29). The Spirit would be with the House of Israel forever.

In these two chapters, Ezekiel has negated the people's fear that God might act against Israel in the future (34:28a). Ezekiel was assured that Israel would always be a holy people, protected against sinning. Therefore, they would never require either divine punishment or announcements of judgment that had characterized the pre-exilic prophets.

Preaching and Teaching Hope from Apocalyptic Ezekiel

Preachers and teachers have the opportunity to proclaim God's word to a holy people as well, for Ezekiel's prophecy has taught them that God will be in charge of all life as long as they are faithful. It has also taught them that God is with them wherever they are and that God will not abandon them. Thus, teachers and preachers live as ambassadors of God's great love for all creation. Ezekiel readings are found in the various lectionaries (see the Appendix). What are some practical ways preachers and teachers can reflect this material to a community?

Plan A

Focus: God is present wherever the holy people are located (Ezek 1–3).

Function: To enable the hearers to understand how they limit the magnitude of God in their own lives and, thus, do not speak of God as inclusive

    I.   God only in the Temple in Jerusalem.
        A. Narrow vision of God.
        B. Why God comes on wheels to Babylon.
    II. Ezekiel's role in bringing God to the people in Babylon.
        A. Meaning of Ezekiel's silent time.
        B. Why he was struck dumb.
        C. God commands Ezekiel to speak when it is time.

III. Where God is in our world today.
   A. How we limit the place of God.
   B. How we move with hope toward a more inclusive God.
   C. How we speak that vision in God's time.

Plan B

Focus: We are hopeful people because we trust in God's compassionate care (Ezek 1–3).

Function: To enable the hope-filled hearers to be more trustful of God in their own lives

   I. Ezekiel's bleak vision at first.
      A. Need to recognize his human limitations.
      B. Must allow God to speak through him.
   II. How change happened for Ezekiel.
      A. Ezekiel was open to the visions.
      B. He began to trust in God's goodness.
   III. How our vision is hopeful today.
      A. Need for an attitude of trust in order to build God's reign.
      B. Need to allow God to sustain us as hope-filled people of trust.

Plan C

Focus: We are weak people when we refuse to live with eyes of justice (Ezek 38–39).

Function: To enable the hearers to contemplate the connection between their own weakness and their inability to see the need for justice in our world

   I. Israelites had not connected exile with their inability to live the covenant.
      A. Ezekiel prophesies divine opposition to their enemies.
      B. Nevertheless, some people remain complacent toward God's ways.

II. God is fully in control.
  A. People fear God's mighty ways.
  B. God's display of holiness changes their hearts.

III. Recognition of weakness in God's people today.
  A. How actions of justice are connected to God.
  B. How many are complacent toward God's justice and mercy in our world.
  C. People can hope in God's holiness to move from weakness to open eyes of justice.

Plan D

Focus: God's mercy is what helps us win life's battles (Ezek 38–39).

Function: To enable the hearers to go beyond the battle language of the Bible and to see that God is merciful because the hearers are actors in the plan of God

I. Graphic description of battle in the biblical text.
  A. How the biblical people understood God as fighting their battles.
  B. Bible shows not *how* God acts but *that* God acts.

II. Israel is defenseless without God.
  A. God acts in spite of their defenselessness.
  B. Their perspective is that God uses the people to win the battle.
  C. They are shown that God acts on their behalf because of God's mercy, not because of what they accomplish.

III. God in our battles today.
  A. With confidence in God, we realize our own defenselessness.
  B. God's mercy overwhelms evil, but justice people act against this evil.
  C. We hope in God's continued mercy in the battles against evil in our own lives.

This is what we are about:
We plant seeds that one day will grow.
We water seeds already planted,
knowing that they hold future promise
We provide yeast that produces
effects beyond our capabilities.
                    —*Attributed to Oscar Romero*[1]

Chapter Seven

UNMASKING APOCALYPTIC LITERATURE: ZECHARIAH, DANIEL

While hosting an Iraqi Dominican sister during summer 2000, the Grand Rapids Dominican Sisters were richly, but painfully, blessed. She spoke simply: "Over 100,000 Iraqis, mostly children, have died because of United Nations sanctions. Please help change your United States foreign policy."

On September 11, 2001, when apocalyptic-like disaster befell the United States, it was ironic that the first of many messages from Dominicans came from the superior in Iraq: "It was with sadness that we heard of the disaster. Having experienced such devastating attacks, we can imagine how difficult it has been. We are strongly against such a barbaric act of terrorism. You are present in our prayers. Please accept our solidarity and our sympathy on the loss of so many innocent people." The memo poignantly concluded, "May God's work overcome the evil throughout the world."[2] Even though tragic suffering is an everyday experience for these sisters, a stance toward life that is rooted in faith and resolutely centered in hope sustains them.

So that preachers and teachers can move toward that same stance of life during times of crisis, they ought to understand all apocalyptic texts in the lectionary and be able to apply them to today's crises in a hope-filled way. In this chapter we consider the apocalyptic texts from Zechariah and Daniel.

UNMASKING APOCALYPTIC ZECHARIAH

The second section (Zech 9–14) of this prophetic work is the apocalyptic Zechariah. In Greek, *deutero* means "second." Therefore, Zechariah 9–14 is often called Deutero-Zechariah or Second Zechariah. Scholars have long noted that Zechariah's focus dramatically shifts between chapters 8 and 9, which could imply different authors or a different time period.

Zechariah's Community in Crisis

The historical background for the prophet who wrote the first eight chapters suggests the reason for Zechariah's prophetic labors. Cyrus of Persia decreed (536 BCE) that the exiles could return to Jerusalem. Since *Zechariah* in Hebrew means "YHWH Remembers," the role of this prophet in the return may be highlighted by name. How many people followed this edict and immediately returned to Jerusalem and what attitude they carried with them is uncertain.

In the second month of 535 BCE, a foundation was laid for the new Temple (Ezra 3:11–13). Immediately, conflict broke out between the Jews and Samaritans, which led to a fourteen-year standstill. Conflict was likely because, according to the returned Jews, the Samaritans were a heretical and schismatic group of spurious worshippers of the God of Israel. They were detested even more than pagans. The origins of this Samaritan/Jewish schism probably reflect the fact that Israel (northern tribes) and Judah were never united. Political and religious divisions appear both before the rules of David and Solomon (1000–960 BCE, 961–922 BCE) and after the establishment of the realm of Israel by

Jeroboam I (922–901 BCE) and the realm of Judah under Rehoboam (922–915 BCE).

In 521 BCE, Darius Hystaspis petitioned Haggai and Zechariah to encourage the people to continue the rebuilding. The prophets probably accomplished this by shaming the Israelites who had built their own homes before they built the Temple. Work went forth under the leadership of Joshua and Zerubbabel, but another short delay resulted with the change of Persian rulers.

Haggai and Zechariah spoke boldly of the people's indifference to their covenant responsibility of rebuilding the Temple. As a result, God moved the Israelites' spirits to complete the Temple by 515 BCE. Haggai's chief purpose was the rebuilding of the Temple itself, while Zechariah's goal was a complete spiritual renewal of the people. Zechariah's ministry was more complex, for it touched upon the intangible reality of a complacent and lethargic attitude.

Given this background, we can ask what situation motivated a second prophet to write a new style work that was very different from the earlier chapters? Opposition to the reconstruction of the Temple and the walls of Jerusalem no longer troubled Israel. But, had the people again become complacent? The prophet depicts an enormous invasion that would sweep away all hostile neighbors: Tyre, Ashkelon, Gaza, and Ekron. There may be a double application to this invasion. First, the invasion sets forth the past judgment upon the kingdoms surrounding Israel, and second, it shows that future punishment awaits the enemies of God's people that will be living in land contiguous to Palestine.

Zechariah's Words of Hope

The apocalyptic material of Zechariah 9–14 moves away from the particular (building a temple) and embraces the universal. These chapters contain divine oracles, prophetic sayings, poetry, indictment of foreign nations, call to communal lament, and language of both woe toward foreign nations and weal toward the House of God. The literary devices attest to the activity of individuals as mediators of the divine world to humanity.

The defeat of all the enemies of Israel is the essence of these chapters. Zechariah 9 begins with God's actions against the Syro-Palestinian territory. On the one hand, Paul Redditt recognizes this writing as characteristic of biblical holy war thinking in which the success of the whole battle is attributed to God.[3] Indeed, the ancient covenant people believed that God would protect Israel in all their battles, so why would it be written any other way? Paul Hanson, on the other hand, claims that there is no human conqueror but that the author is merely showing God's reestablishment of the time-honored boundaries of Israel in its greatest time of glory.[4]

Zechariah prophesies peace with a king who arrives, with splendid procession and shouts of rejoicing, in the city (9:9). This language is very familiar to Christians, who affirm the fulfillment of the prophecy again and again each Palm Sunday, when they hear the text of Jesus riding into Jerusalem on a young colt (see Mark 11:2ff). The symbolism indicates God's plan for permanent and lasting peace. Preachers and teachers can express hope that there will be a mighty agent of peace, who has a humble and lowly spirit.

Zechariah 10 expresses Israel's promises, contrasting their future blessedness with their past disobedience. In this new age, they need only ask and God provides rain for vegetation, compassion for themselves and others, and strength from this God who loves them. God may still be "hot against the shepherds and...leaders" (10:3), but God also promises to "strengthen the house of Judah...and save the house of Joseph." The compassionate God will always bring them back (10:6a,b).

Zechariah 11 inaugurates a poetic drama, using an array of images to act out a scene.

- God orders the doors of Lebanon opened, so fire can enter to destroy the cedars. (Cedars of Lebanon in the scriptures portray the proud—powerful kings are often the targets. See Ps 29:5; Judg 9:15; Isa 2:13, 14:8.)
- The returnees from Babylon come into the land (10:10).
- The "cypress" and the "oaks of Bashan" wail as symbols of ruling power. (The word used for "trees" in all these passages metaphorically suggests majestic kings and powerful nations. See Judg 9:8–15; Ezek 31.)

- The powerful shepherd experiences grievous ruin (see Jer 25:34–37).
- The leaders roar like lions when the pride of Jordan is destroyed. (See Prov 19:12, 20:2, where "a king's anger is like the growling of a lion.")

The *NRSV* expresses most clearly the relation between Zechariah 11, verses 2 and 3. A twofold command to wail in 11:2 is matched by the twofold command to listen in 11:3. One might imagine the command to wail followed instantly by the reverberation of wailing.

The chapter continues with a cryptic picture of the worthless shepherd. This text is difficult, for it contains a grim development of events and suggests a peculiar logic now impenetrable. God orders Zechariah to be a shepherd so that he may take care of the "flock doomed to slaughter" (11:7b). It appears that Zechariah is doing God's work (9:16a), for God is often "the one who shepherds" (see Gen 48:15; Ps 79:13; Mic 7:14). Appearances do not always count, however, for the impatient shepherd Zechariah destroys the irresponsible and unfaithful shepherds.

Unfortunately, he also turns against the sheep, saying, "I will not be your shepherd. Let the dying die, and the perishing perish" (11:9a). However, Zechariah's disgust cannot stop him from being God's shepherd. He picks up two staffs, symbolically naming them "Favor" and "Unity" and breaks the staff called Favor, which annuls the covenant made with the people (11:10). The sheep merchants, watching this agonizing scene, understand that the prophetic sign refers to breaking covenant with God (11:11).

Afterward, Zechariah dares to ask the merchants for a shepherd's wage, but is given an insulting amount—thirty shekels of silver (11:12c). So, God tells Zechariah to cast the wages into the treasury, for "this Lordly price" (11:13) is an insult to God. The strength of this passage is that thirty shekels is the price of a slave (Exod 21:32), so, in essence, Zechariah is deemed their slave. "Lordly price" is meant to be ironic, and Zechariah's action reprimands the people for paying such a low wage. This same amount is picked up as the wage earned by Judas for turning Jesus over to the authorities (Matt 26:15).

Then Zechariah breaks the staff Unity, "annulling the family ties between Judah and Israel" (11:14). The ending feels like absolute destruction, with the shepherd devouring his own sheep (11:16) and then being cursed by God as a worthless shepherd (11:17). The potent language of Zechariah 11, however, reveals several things:

- Zechariah speaks in the first person (11:4), uttering, "Thus said the Lord my God."
- The people had been wandering like sheep without a shepherd (10:1–2). Now the shepherd is condemned and the sheep (people; see 10:2–3) are purchased for slaughter.
- Purchasing sheep is a punishable offense, but the shepherds are left to gloat: "I have become rich" (11:5b), contrasted with the paltry sum Zechariah was paid (11:12–13).
- Earth represents all the land being "won" by God (9: 1–8) so that the exiles may come back into the land (10:10).
- God's threat is overwhelming: "I will cause them…to fall each into the hand of a neighbor,…and I will deliver no one from their hand" (11:6b, c). Punishment for not living the covenant is more severe than the people might have originally assumed. (See 2 Sam 3:8 for "handing over to the enemy" and Amos 1:2–2:3 for "crimes that go unpunished.")
- Zechariah 11:7 has a different feel when one reads from the *Tanakh*, the English translation of the Hebrew Bible: "So I tended the sheep meant for slaughter, for those poor men of the sheep I got two staffs" (10:2).

"Hopeless shepherds and hopeless sheep" might be an image that summarizes this chapter. Shepherds are hopeless because they don't care for their sheep. Sheep are hopeless because they are used to bring wealth to some who have bartered the living of the covenant for it. Zechariah's shepherding seems to involve both. Nevertheless, God still prefers the lands of Judah and Ephraim—another name for Israel—to other lands in the Ancient Near East where returnees might dwell (Zech 9).

The closing oracle in chapter 11 presents a picture of an annulled covenant, for ties have been broken between Judah and

Israel. This break results in God's rhetorical question, "Even though it seems impossible to the remnant of this people in these days, should it also seem impossible to me?" (8:6).

The Jewish leaders and people alike called a grand view of the future into question. They had a rebuilt Temple, but Zechariah's work was only worth "thirty pieces of silver" (11:12b). The dealings of both shepherd and sheep in Zechariah 11 have undermined the hyperbolic claims about the centrality of power in the Temple in Jerusalem (see 8:22). These dealings are rooted in the question of Jerusalem "on that day" (12:3a). Zechariah knows that the people's only hope is in God, so his language becomes even more exaggerated.

Notice how the spotlight is on Judah as well as Israel (Northern Kingdom) in chapter 12. Zechariah proclaims that God is going to make Jerusalem a "cup of reeling for all the surrounding peoples" (12:2a).[5] This imagery seems to highlight a Jerusalem that causes nations to stagger as if intoxicated. God is angry and will pour wrath upon the foreigners and even upon Israel (see Isa 51:17 and Jer 25:15–16 for similar images).

Nevertheless, this action affects Judah as well. The Holy One will watch it (12:4b), and so the clans of Judah can proclaim in faith that the Lord of Hosts has strengthened them (12:5). Thus, when the enemy comes to fight, Judah will be a rampart around Jerusalem (see also 9:3).

Zechariah imagines God dominating the nations so that people in Judah will open their eyes and focus upon God. The leaders of Jerusalem "say in their hearts" (12:5a, *REB*) that they are required to live their covenant with God in order to restrain God's anger. Earlier God was described as a "wall of fire" around Jerusalem (2:1–5). Here Judah swiftly disappears, and the focus is upon Jerusalem (12:8). A fenced-in Jerusalem, protected from the outside world, is the very opposite of the Jerusalem "inhabited like villages without walls" (Zech 2:4b).

In the scene that describes what will happen in those days, the feeblest are compared to the house of David—an image likened to God. Zechariah's status and God's power have grown exponentially. The oracle paints a different picture of God now. From one who has plundered the nations (2:9), God seeks now to preserve

Jerusalem against all the nations (12:9). The other nations will not be harmed if they don't interfere.

Zechariah 12:10–14 probably describes the final eschatological conflict that was prophesied to happen in the plain of Megiddo (12:11). The battle and the cleansing from sin lead directly into a profound description of what will happen on that day. All evil will be destroyed and the *Day of the Lord* will dawn. Then God will become king over all the earth, and God's name will be one (14: 9).

God's return as Zechariah describes it is not one of disinterested compassion. The central message is that God will be in Jerusalem with God's holy people forever. This message might seem like a radical localization of the divine to us. But we have to take the message a step further and look at the *reason* for God's anger. There is too much emphasis on wealth and prosperity surrounding the Temple rebuilding, so God negates the Temple and emphasizes a time in the future with no Temple.

Preaching and Teaching Hope from Apocalyptic Zechariah

Like Zechariah, preachers and teachers are still confronted by the challenge of asking critical questions about the Jerusalem of their lives. In other words, what is the place of God in their lives? Has self-interest engulfed them? Has self-interest drained their spirits of passion for God? These questions are as relevant today as in the time of Zechariah. They are asked in hope—for they move teachers and preachers to *let go and let God*. See the Appendix for these Zechariah readings. Some specific outlines might help in preaching and teaching hope from Deutero-Zechariah.

Plan A

Focus: We live with hope when we participate in God's victory over the forces of evil (Zech 9–10).

Function: To enable the hearers to understand that it takes prayerful discernment to realize the underlying causes of evil in our world and not just the evil itself

I. Holy war language within scripture.
   A. People might interpret biblical "holy war" text as God's victory for us alone.
   B. Problem: attributing human action to God.

II. God's protection within the scriptures.
   A. Bible written from point of view of the victor (Israel).
   B. Israel believes that God is protecting them throughout their history.
   C. What that means about protection of other people.

III. God's protection of us brings us to hopeful living and involves us in destroying the forces of evil.
   A. We are God's people when we assist in the destruction of evil.
   B. How we begin to interpret what is evil around us.
   C. Hopefulness calls us to prayerful discernment about the concept of evil.

Plan B

Focus: We live hopefully in covenant with God, but not at the expense of favor over unity (Zech 11).

Function: To enable the hearers to see how they have broken their covenant with God and that only God can repair it; but God will repair it through our good actions

I. God's covenant is broken.
   A. Zechariah breaks the staff named Favor and also asks for a just wage.
   B. Both are symbolic, reprimanding the people for not living the covenant they made with God; do they realize this?

II. Can covenant with God be repaired?
   A. By themselves, people can do nothing to make reparation.

    B. Israel has a rebuilt Temple, but God seems absent or angry because the people have fenced themselves in.

    C. God's rhetorical question: Is reparation impossible for me?

III. Covenant with God continues through us.

    A. We cannot live in a fenced-in Jerusalem either.

    B. God will favor us, if we become frail before God and realize that God uses us to act in justice.

    C. Hope necessitates unity, not favor, to seek justice.

Plan C

Focus: We are to imagine with hope the Day of the Lord (Zech 12–14).

Function: To enable the hearers to imagine a day without sin and evil and with mercy and justice

I. Preparation for the Day of the Lord.

    A. All must be cleansed from sin to participate.

    B. What would it look like if all evil were destroyed?

II. The Day of the Lord in Jerusalem.

    A. The Temple, surrounded with wealth and prosperity, is not ready for the Day of the Lord.

    B. On the Day of the Lord, there will not be need for a temple.

III. How will we recognize the Day of the Lord?

    A. How will we recognize the temples that we keep grasping?

    B. The question of self-interest versus the spirit of compassion, mercy, and justice.

    C. The ability to "Let go and let God."

    D. This ability will lead us with hope to the Day of the Lord.

UNMASKING THE APOCALYPTIC DANIEL

Most people have had dreams. Maybe the dreams have been frightening. But people often learn something about their unconscious from a dream, some message for their lives. This hope has led many to record their dreams immediately after waking. So, too, Daniel's dreams (visions) were a constant companion to him. These dreams are the crowning jewels of First Testament apocalyptic passages, for Daniel has always been identified as apocalyptic literature.

The prophet Habakkuk describes Daniel's process and, perhaps, the process for all people when he says that we are to

Write the vision;
    make it plain on tablets,
    so that a runner may read it.
For there is still a vision for the appointed time;
    it speaks of the end, and does not lie.
If it seems to tarry, wait for it;
    it will surely come; it will not delay. (Hab 2:2–3)

Someone named Daniel took this advice seriously and launches readers into the apocalyptic study of the written visions recorded in Daniel 7–12.

Daniel's Community in Crisis

Scholars agree that the vision section (Dan 7–12) belongs to a time of crisis when the Jewish people needed encouragement to focus upon their inherited tradition. Antiochus Epiphanes, who wished to impose the Greek Hellenistic culture upon the Jews, initiated the crisis of faith.

Before the accession of Antiochus, there was a strong movement in favor of Hellenism among the wealthy and the priestly aristocracy of Jerusalem. Because of the initiative of this group, Antiochus permitted the building of a gymnasium in Jerusalem (see 1 Macc 1:11). This wealthy and priestly aristocracy wished to abandon the religious and cultural traditions of Israel and assimilate the nation to Hellenistic civilization. The majority of Jews resisted this movement because it aggravated already strained relations. The author of Daniel was also reacting against imposing Hellenism upon his people. Other books from this period, for example 1 Maccabees, describe this Jewish tension in greater detail.

It is important to focus upon the fact that Antiochus Epiphanes succeeded in finding Jews who would promote Hellenistic living. These people tended to put aside their religion because of the pressure exerted and the incentives offered. Nevertheless, 1 Maccabees also claims that many resisted. This Jewish struggle brought about horrendous actions against the populace: desecration of their Temple sanctuary, suppression of religious festivals and three and one-half years of extremely inhumane suffering. The author of Daniel recognized these extreme pressures and, from dreams given him, wrote God's message to these faithful ones.

Coded language was used—for example, various kinds of beasts to represent evil—so if the book fell into the hands of government leaders, the Jews would not be considered guilty of subversion. It is quite reasonable to assume that government leaders could not break the codes, but that the author's intended meaning was clear to the Jews who knew their biblical heritage.

Daniel's Words of Hope

Daniel 7–12 concerns itself with the destinies of humankind under God's control. God's sovereignty is not evident in this text except through special revelations to the *maśkīlīm*. These are accompanied by strange acts of deliverance. They take on special significance as a result of persecutions by Antiochus Epiphanes in 167 BCE. The Gentile kingdoms at this time were not known as loyal servants of God. Instead, they initiated voluminous evil and were known as insubordinate monsters that needed to be destroyed.

Daniel 7 has immense evocative power and visions bursting with symbolism. Four kingdoms are pictured as beasts coming out of the sea. In ancient mythological tradition, the sea is always the place of chaos. The beasts coming from it are monsters representing evil (see Isa 27:1 and Ps 74:13).[6] Thus, the kingdoms are pictured as grotesque eruptions amidst chaos. It is no wonder that Daniel was "terrified by the visions of his mind" (7:1b). He had to develop a flourishing imagination in order to appreciate the visions. The teacher and preacher of Daniel will also need a vivid imagination to portray these visions adequately.

There is a certain sense of divine providence when the scene changes to one of heavenly majesty, with the Ancient One on the throne and, later, one like a *son of man* coming on the clouds (7:8ff.). There are at least two levels of interpretation: (1) how the imagery had already been used, and (2) its use in the context under consideration.[7] Daniel illuminates the situation of the Jews under Antiochus Epiphanes, but the imagery obscures the particular historical situation and thrusts it into a universal pattern. Although Gentile rulers have their way in the persecution taking place, the traditional imagery implies an inevitable judgment: the monsters of chaos will be overcome by one like the son of man, who takes the place of Baal, the most noted pagan god. This imagery brings hope to the Jewish people, who believe that they will prevail.

The mysterious identity of the son of man makes the content provocative. Scholars are divided concerning this identity. McKenzie remarks that some scholars connect the "son of man" with a figure of Iranian mythology called "Primordial Man," the first man who is deified and who will return in the final period of the world to inaugurate the kingdom of God. It seems that the only merit of this theory is the patterning after a specific person. Nevertheless, it is evident that the son of man has at least three different identities:

1. The son of man could be symbolic of God's saving action among the people.
2. The son of man could be the corporate figure of the Jewish people.
3. The son of man could be the Messiah they expected.

In the end, the son of man is probably that special individual who invites others to identify and act in his mission as Messiah. That mysterious quality, no proper names given, seems to specify that it is not important to identify the son of man but only to recognize that, because of this son of man, the heavenly one embraces the covenant community.

A puzzling point concerns the use of the "holy ones." The Hebrew Bible uses this term primarily for angels or supernatural beings, but here the phrase seems to be used for the covenant community (7:18). A possible solution offered by Collins is that the precedence of the world of the gods is assumed, while earthly matters are taken as a reflection of this superior reality. This clarifies the relationship of the heavenly holy ones to the people of the earth, as the text states:

> The greatness of the kingdoms under the whole heaven
>   shall be given to the people of the holy ones of the Most High. (7:27)

Chapter 8 of the Book of Daniel is divided into two parts: (1) a complex vision utilizing animal imagery instead of four kingdoms (8:1–14) and (2) the interpretation by the angel sent from God (8:15–26). Scholars generally agree that the charging ram with two long horns represents the Medo-Persian kingdom that dominated Judah with power, and the he-goat refers to the reign of Alexander the Great of Greece, who will overthrow the Persian Empire. The one little horn that grew from one of the four horns was allowed to flourish, while the four horns diminished. This little horn represents Antiochus, who became ruler through the Seleucids in Egypt.

The predominant concern of Daniel 9 is how to interpret a Jeremiah passage that described the time of exile as seventy weeks (see Jer 25:11–12, 29:10). However, the chapter begins with a *communal* prayer of confession on the lips of Daniel. The prayer shows that the Hebrew people are being punished for their sin, which will be removed when they repent and pray. Yet, it is clear to the reader of the text that heaven was not listening to Daniel's prayer, for Gabriel had been sent to help him understand.

The theology of the prayer, common in the liturgy at the synagogue, seems to be in sharp contrast to the apocalyptic framework of Daniel. As the prayer ends, however, Daniel realizes that the plan of deliverance had been decreed separately from Daniel's pleas for forgiveness. What Daniel needed was wisdom and understanding (9:22). This led him to recognize that seventy years meant seventy weeks of years (that is, a very long time). In the first seven weeks the people came home to Jerusalem, and in the next sixty-two weeks they rebuilt their city and the Temple.

The last and most exciting week inaugurates the end times, when the final restitution takes place. Perhaps Daniel's vision of seventy weeks once offered a theory of history that Christian chroniclers found amiable to their own, where events preceding the end of the age could be placed according to a conveniently determined plan. Nevertheless, in spite of this new understanding, Daniel's purpose is not to speculate about the future but to provide assurance that the predetermined period of Gentile sovereignty is coming to an end.

It is often suggested that Daniel 10–12 is an entire historical apocalypse in the form of an epiphany delivered by an angel (see Ezek 1:8–10 and Rev 1:13–15). The introduction shows the shift from the reign of Cyrus of Persia to Antiochus Epiphanes. Then the manifestation of God is incorporated within an elaborate apocalypse. This writing accounts the seer's state of affairs and his preferences. An angelic discourse fills in the text until the end of these three chapters.

These chapters differ from a prophetic commissioning in two ways:

1. The message is not a brief oracle but a long prediction of events to come.
2. The seer writes the message down instead of proclaiming it and seals the book until the end time when the events will come to pass.

A striking difference is that the wise will read and understand the message as relevant for their own time and will also understand it in relation to the end time.

As chapter 12 begins, Daniel is fasting and mourning. Notice that this type of preparation is often part of the preparation for receiving a vision. The mourning probably includes the prayer that begins chapter 9. After Daniel's preparation, he hears a recitation of selected events in various stages of history from the Macedonian kingdom to the time of Antiochus III. He knows that the end is near and the fall of the wicked is certain (11:40).

Eventually, Michael the Archangel, the guardian of the people, proclaims that those whose names are written in the book will escape disaster. The seer Daniel seals the book until the time of the end. The curious ones wish to predict the number of years until that end. However, the holy people are encouraged to have patience and persevere, for eventually they shall rise for their reward at the end of time (12:12–13). They need not be concerned about the number of years.

Daniel's imaginative presentation brings hope by allowing the Jewish people to cope with the crisis of persecution in three distinct ways:

1. By helping them clearly identify the vastness of the evil confronting them
2. By supplying assurance that the evil force will, in time, be overcome by a higher power
3. By providing a skeleton of action that supports those who lay down their lives as faithful witnesses

Preaching and Teaching Hope from Apocalyptic Daniel

Recognizing evil, supplying certainty, overpowering evil forces, witnessing by action—these are unquestionably sources of hope for a people suffering the wrath of persecution.

They are hopeful words for preachers and teachers alike, who need to recognize the enormity of evil all around that is trying to sway the faithful ones from basic values and beliefs. First, preachers and teachers ought to have hope that a loving God will overcome the evil forces on this earth and be ready to preach and teach this hope. People need to be reminded that there are many martyrs even today. Among them are those who stand up for truth in relation to Third World debt, those who lay down their lives to bring food to starving people in Iraq, and those who fight the U.S. government's buildup of arms against ghost enemies. There are also many others who witness in ordinary ways at the United Nations, in the halls of justice, in schools and churches. The Book of Daniel gives hope to all these courageous people that God is with them in their pursuit of holiness. See the Appendix for readings within the various lectionaries. Following I suggest ways that the hope of these apocalyptic chapters might be taught and preached.

Plan A

Focus: We must ready ourselves to approach the end times with hope (Dan 7).

Function: To enable the hearers to realize that, if they are to be counted among God's holy ones, they might have to suffer persecution in order for the end times to emerge

 I. Text description is a universal pattern of the end times.
  A. Ancient One on the throne.
  B. Son of man coming on the clouds.

 II. The final destruction of evil will not happen all at once.
  A. Gentile rulers seem to prevail over Israel.
  B. Destruction of evil involves persecution of the holy ones.
  C. Inevitable judgment of the evil ones.

 III. The Heavenly One embraces the covenant community.
  A. We cannot assume we are part of the covenant community.
  B. We might have to suffer the ignominy of those who are yet too prideful and make decisions that cause persecution of the holy ones.
  C. We must live with justice and peace at the forefront of our lives.
  D. If we live in this way, we can hope in God's mercy.

Plan B

Focus: The beasts from the sea must be attacked with hope in God (Dan 8).

Function: To enable the hearers to recognize their own beasts from the sea and to relate these to social beasts that might have caused crises.

I.   Ancient mythological tradition about beasts from the sea.
   A. The sea is a fearsome place. (Refer to a maritime disaster that is well known and remembered locally; for example, the *Andrea Doria* in the Atlantic Ocean, 1956; *Edmund Fitzgerald* on Lake Superior, 1975; MSS *Estonia* in the Baltic, 1994; the Staten Island Ferry in New York, 2003; the tsunami in the Indian Ocean, 2004.)
   B. The beasts always represent evil.

II.   Daniel's visions of these beasts.
   A. Use of imagination in reading such texts.
   B. They symbolically represent the enemies of Judah in the second century BCE.

III. The beasts in our own lives.
   A. Recognizing the beasts from the sea in our own lives.
   B. What we have learned since September 11, 2001, about evil in us and in our world.
   C. How we contribute to social evil and how we maintain hope in God in spite of that continuing evil.

Plan C

Focus: It is necessary to pray communally to engender hope of God's glory (Dan 9).

Function: To enable the hearers to confess their own need for repentance in some social format and to pray for wisdom and understanding concerning the continued evils of our society

I. Confession on the lips of Daniel is interpreted as a communal prayer of all the people.
   A. Shows the covenant people being punished for their sins.
   B. Punishment will be removed when they prayerfully repent.

II. From the prayer, Daniel is given wisdom and understanding.
   A. David understands the seventy weeks.
   B. The seventy weeks lead them to the end times.
      1. 7 weeks: People come home to Jerusalem.
      2. 62 weeks: They rebuild the city and the Temple.
      3. Last week: Inaugurates the end times.

III. Our communal prayer today.
   A. We must have an attitude of repentance.
   B. We will be given wisdom and understanding.
   C. We hope that we will contribute to the elimination of social evil and that God will bring us to glory in the end times.

Plan D

Focus: We fast and mourn in order for God to reign in glory among us (Dan 12–14).

Function: To enable the hearers to see, within the context of history, the problems that have led to social ills and have kept the end times from coming upon us

I. Daniel fasts and mourns.
   A. This prepares Daniel for receiving a vision from God.
   B. The vision is a recitation of selected events from various stages of history.
   C. Daniel knows that the end is near and the fall of the wicked is certain.

II. Michael the Archangel inaugurates the end by reciting the names of those written in God's book.

    A. This action is symbolic of the separation of good and evil.

    B. Some people don't see the symbolism and wish, instead, to know when all these things will happen.

    C. The holy ones are encouraged to have patience and to persevere.

    D. Then they will be ready for God's glory.

III. What we must do in order for God to reign among us.

    A. Fasting and mourning must be a part of our prayer lives.

    B. This will assist us in seeing how the good is separated from the evil.

    C. We live in hope that our lives have been holy enough to have our names written in God's book.

    D. This kind of hope means that we have been patient and have persevered in acting justly and rightly before God.

    E. Then we will not fear, but we, too, will be ready for God's glory to come among us.

CONCLUSION

A professor once said that God doesn't call prophets to be successful but only faithful. This chapter has implied that, as the world counts it, prophetic apocalyptic writers were not successful. More often than not, their messages fell on deaf ears. Nonetheless, they remained faithful. Deaf ears today might be those able to hear but not listening for God's way. Faithful preachers and teachers are needed to proclaim the apocalyptic message that God will, ultimately, win over all evil. The Spirit of God is reliable and will lift people out of many kinds of death and into new life.

We move now to chapters 8 through 10, which investigate the apocalyptic writers of the Second Testament and how they provided hope and lifted their communities out of death. Specific examples of how to preach and teach those texts are given.

Hope does not disappoint us,
because God's love
has been poured into our hearts
through the Holy Spirit
that has been given to us.
                    —*Romans 5:5*

Chapter Eight

UNMASKING APOCALYPTIC LITERATURE: 1 AND 2 THESSALONIANS

The Second Testament, by its very nature as texts that emerged from the crisis of the beginnings of the first-century Christian church, has a hope-filled apocalyptic tone throughout. Early Christians struggled with the fact that Jesus came into the Jewish world but the actions and words of Jesus interested Gentiles to begin following his ways as well. These followers of Jesus had been stunned that he was put to death in such a gruesome way! One can imagine that early community of followers sinking deeply into despair before emerging in hope that the Christ was still alive and living in the spirit of this new Christian movement.

Although not an apocalyptic text, a prime text for meditation on this struggle of early Christians is that of the disciples walking the road to Emmaus (Luke 24:13–35). These disciples reflected the attitude of many within the Jewish, turned Christian, community. They thought they knew their scriptures. They believed that Jesus had come to save Israel from any further defilement by the Gentiles. How were they to understand the death of Jesus, his rising, and then this new wave of Gentile belief?

The risen one that appeared in their midst conversed with them and subsequently reprimanded them for not knowing their scriptures. Their eyes were opened and their hearts burned when they recognized him in the breaking of the bread. This appearance, among others, convinced these early followers of Jesus that they had to return to their scriptures to find significance to the life, death, and resurrection of Jesus.

During the next twenty years, at least until the time of Paul, many of these Christians lived in a community of common sharing. As Luke idealizes it, they sold their possessions so that all in the community had what they needed in order to live. Luke also relates that they broke bread in their homes, but they still went to the synagogue to praise God (see Acts 2:43–47). These early Christians were still very Jewish, until the influx of Gentiles. As Luke describes in Acts 15, there had to be some negotiation about these Gentile converts.

We are indebted to the greatest preacher and teacher of the early church for a picture of the struggles and the growth of these early Christian communities. Paul's letters, both the seven that are authentically written by Paul and those of early followers who wrote in the name of Paul,[1] were historically the first written texts of the Second Testament.

In this chapter of apocalyptic overview, we look at Paul's earliest letter to the community at Thessalonica, perhaps written 50–52 BCE, as well as the second letter to that community, either written by Paul at a later date or by one of his followers. These Pauline letters will be unmasked to assist readers, preachers, and teachers who encounter these texts within the various lectionaries, who choose to teach this material in a class, or who choose to preach the texts during a time of crisis. Readers and preachers might imagine they are walking that journey to Emmaus, allowing their hearts to burn in many ways as they dig deeply into the Second Testament apocalyptic literature.

Their hearts might burn when they recognize the risen Christ in the stranger on the road, when they move from disbelief to belief because of the love of that stranger among them, when they open the scriptures and allow Jesus to interpret for them in prayer, when they are hospitable to the strangers who come into their path, and last, when they, too, recognize Jesus in the breaking of the bread. This preparation with the spirit of faith will move imaginative readers, preachers, and teachers with hope toward action on behalf of justice and peace. In the end, then, the goal of this chapter, along with chapters 9 and 10, is to journey toward hope and away from despair in the same way that the early Christians did.

ABOUT LETTERS FROM PAUL'S PERSPECTIVE

A major shift must be made when reading the letters of the Second Testament. Since a significant portion of both testaments is narrative, the reader must make a shift to the style of letter. Letters cannot be read in the same way as narrative or story, where we look for plot, characterization, and dramatic movement. Letters are one-way communication, like listening to one side of a phone conversation and trying to discern the other person's words. Thus, Paul is answering questions and making comments to a given community about issues that community is facing, concerns that we only know with insights about the given community.

It is important that readers find out about the community being addressed and, then, situating themselves within its membership, make educated responses to Paul. Paul's message is a very important way of responding to that community, but it is not the only way. Readers should not be afraid to question Paul as they read, because Paul himself might have discussed the issues with members of the communities if he had been "face to face" with them.

What, then, was Paul's purpose for writing letters? He wrote before any Gospels were written (50–63 CE), so he was not attempting to circulate the story of Jesus. In fact, Paul knew the story of Jesus so well that he assumed those in his fledgling communities also knew the story. Paul's goal was to *persuade* the community members to live like Jesus.

We can think about arguments of persuasion by studying how television commercials achieve their goal of persuasion. Four questions are probably asked:

1. What are we trying to accomplish?
2. What audience are we addressing?
3. What message needs to be given in order to reach that audience?
4. How will we know if the commercial has been successful?

Those editing commercials might answer: (1) We want to sell the product and, in the end, the "company"; (2) we know that the audience depends upon the time of day and kind of program; (3) we show how our product is better than any other product on the market; and (4) if the commercial does its job, sales rise.

We can think of Paul, the persuader, answering these same four questions: (1) He wanted to "sell" Christianity as a way of life and to "sell" himself as a credible messenger of that way; (2) his audience were particular Christian communities in the Gentile world with their own unique problems; (3) he wanted to say that they could imitate his as one that imitated the life Jesus intended for his followers; and (4) Paul was successful if he could form a vibrant Christian community.

Once Paul was sure that persuasion worked, he probably posed two other questions. The first, a question of belief, asked why they should believe that Jesus was the way of life, the truth, and the life (John 14:6). The second, a question of action, asked how they were living as followers of Jesus. In summary, Paul might have asked, "If you call yourself Christian, how do others know that you are one?" The popular folk song probably states the answer best: "They'll Know We Are Christians by Our Love."

Paul's experience of Christianity is *passionate*. It is colored by his personal experience of seeing the risen Jesus and being commissioned as apostle to the Gentiles (see Gal 2:7; Phil 1:30; and Rom 11:13). Thus, readers of his letters must embrace Paul's conviction and read the letters with *heart* more than *head*. They are encouraged to look for metaphors that help them discover the deeper meaning Paul intended to communicate.

Last, readers are reminded that Paul's perspective in his letters was colored by three realities: (1) his understanding of the religious traditions, both Jewish and Christian, of the people embracing this new way of life; (2) Paul's own life experiences and the life experiences of the various communities he visited; and (3) the Jewish and Greek (Hellenist) cultural milieu of that biblical era.

A speaker once indicated that readers of Paul's letters could give three possible responses. Readers could say "Yeh," indicating that they agree with Paul about the issue that they think is being addressed. Second, readers could respond with "Nay" if they disagree with Paul's conclusions regarding a certain issue. A third response for readers of Paul could be "Huh" if they read something that Paul is addressing but Paul's argument becomes extremely technical with Greek comparatives (see 1 Cor 15).

These letters will always be divorced from the reader's experience, but they need not be cold and sterile. The letters became part of the canon because early church leaders understood that some of what Paul said was more universal and could speak to other times. However, care must be taken when applying Paul's ideas to today's problems. These comments on letters allow for the transition into the apocalyptic Paul in the letters to the Thessalonians.

UNMASKING APOCALYPTIC PAUL AT THESSALONICA

Paul's Thessalonian Community in Crisis

Paul loves this community at Thessalonica, which is shown by the length of the thanksgiving section in his first letter (1:2–3:13). He is optimistic and gentle, relishing in the fact that this community was not torn by internal strife. Paul says in tender compassion, "So deeply do we care for you that we…wish to share not only the gospel of God but also our own selves" (1 Thess 1:8).

However, the letter indicates that the Christians in the community expected the *Parousia*, the Greek word for the end times, in their lifetime, and they were worrying about those who already died. Will they share in the Parousia? Perhaps Judaizers, interested in converting Christians back to Judaism, were causing great alarm in the community, preaching and teaching that the Parousia had already occurred.

2 Thessalonians picks up this same theme of the Parousia. However, the writer teaches the community to look for signs that precede the Parousia and then they will be confident of its coming. Thus, both letters show that the community's crisis is a lack of confidence that God will save all in the community, but especially those who had already died.

Paul's Word of Hope

1 Thessalonians is the oldest Christian document in the canon, dated 50–52 CE, only twenty years after Jesus' resurrection. The theological emphasis is encouragement in faith of these converts from paganism. Paul wants to make sure that they are not being led astray because they hear of Paul's persecution and are possibly enduring persecution themselves (see 1 Thess 1:14). Paul is also concerned that they are living upright lives, abstaining from fornication and keeping their bodies holy (1 Thess 4:4). There is encouragement to live in love as they have been taught, being examples of love to all their brothers and sisters. Last, they are to "mind their own affairs" and work diligently in the labor in which they have been trained, so that they earn their living properly (1 Thess 4:11–12).

In this letter, Paul believes that the primary saving event is the Parousia and that he expected it to come upon them soon. So, Paul calms the Thessalonians about their expectations and encourages them to live responsibly in hopefulness while waiting.

Paul reminds the Thessalonians that Jesus Christ died and rose for the salvation of all, and so God will bring to salvation those who have been faithful. The apocalyptic language is found in 1 Thessalonians 4:16–17. Jesus will return at the sound of the God's trumpet, and the dead will rise with Christ to live with God. Then those who are still living will be "caught up in the clouds" and meet the Lord as well. Then, all the faithful will be with God forever.

Paul warns the community that the "day of the Lord will come like a thief in the night" (1 Thess 5:2). Some seem to be emphasizing peace and security, but Paul wants this community to stand its guard, since the suddenness of the Parousia will be like that of a woman in labor pains (1 Thess 5:3). They are encouraged to live as children of the light instead of children of darkness.

Paul suggests that they not fall asleep like others are doing but that they stay awake and sober, living in faith and love and wearing the hope of salvation as their helmets (1 Thess 5:8). Paul is confident that God has destined them "not for wrath but for obtaining salvation" (1 Thess 5:9).

Finally, Paul encourages this community that he loves so dearly to respect the authority of those who labor in the place of the Christ (and surely of Paul). They are to esteem this leadership and learn to live in peace among themselves (1 Thess 5:13). Above all, they are to be patient with all in the community and receive their strength by praying always.[2]

2 Thessalonians is one of three letters that may or may not have been written by Paul.[3] It might have been written by one of his followers, using Paul's style and name for authority. The letter is more impersonal than 1 Thessalonians and seems to reflect a different time period than the earlier letter. The community seems more stressed about the Parousia, thinking of the judgment of God and wondering if they are going to be among the saved.

The writer makes it clear that the Thessalonians can remain hopeful since they are not among those disturbing the community whom God will afflict. The Lord Jesus will mete out "vengeance on those who do not know God and on those who do not obey the Gospel of our Lord Jesus" (2 Thess 1:8). The writer will pray that all in the community might remain worthy of the call of Christ. To accomplish that, members must resolve to work in faith, according to the grace given by God.

The writer warns the community not to be alarmed by those who say that the Day of the Lord has already come. Instead, they should look for the signs that are promised by God. First will come a rebellion, where the lawless one is revealed. God will destroy this lawless one, for he opposes other gods and exalts himself by being seated in the temple of God (2 Thess 2:3–4). The works of Satan manifest this lawless one, who uses wicked deception in order to draw in those who refuse to love the truth (2 Thess 2:10). The deceived will be condemned because of their pleasure in unrighteousness. The community can be hopeful, for when the lawless one appears, he will be immediately removed by the Lord Jesus, who will destroy and annihilate him by the "breath of his mouth" and by the manifestation of his return (2 Thess 2:8).

The community is reminded that they were chosen as the first fruits of salvation, learning the truth from the Spirit. Thus, they are to "stand firm and hold fast to the traditions" they were taught by Paul, either when he visited them or when he wrote a letter (2 Thess 2:15). Paul pleads that these faithful ones be given good hope and eternal comfort in their hearts and that they be strengthened in all good works (2 Thess 2:16–17).

The writer also warns the community to stay away from "believers who are living in idleness." Paul had taught them to work for what they earn, and so busybody community members are reminded to work quietly for their living (2 Thess 3:6–12). The community is to remain alert while doing good works, staying away from those who disobey the letters' commands. These will be ashamed of the way they are living (2 Thess 3:14).

Preaching and Teaching Hope from Apocalyptic Paul

The preaching plans in this section will assist those who preach these letters to the Thessalonians. They emerge in lectionaries, mostly when apocalyptic texts are read (see the Appendix). They may also be chosen as readings during times of crisis. The plans that follow include focus and function statements and a basic structural outline. Using personal and congregational stories will modify them.

Plan A

Focus: Our bodies are holy and they belong to God (1 Thess 4:4).

Function: To enable hearers to broaden their scope concerning healthy sexuality

    I.   Paul encourages the Thessalonians.
        A. Keep your bodies holy.
        B. Refrain from fornication.
        C. Live upright lives.

    II.   Problem for today's Christians.
- A. Lack of modeling from TV, movies, and the Internet.
- B. Lack of modeling from adults.

    III.   Give encouragement and hope to the community.
- A. Elders are true models of holiness for the young.
- B. They must realize the important role they play in the sexual growth of the young.
- C. God calls all to holiness in body as well as soul.
- D. This is true love.

Plan B

Focus: In order to prepare for the Parousia, Christians cannot be idle (1 Thess 4:11–12).

Function: To enable hearers to grow in their talents and how they use them

    I.   Paul teaches the community to live diligently.
- A. Members of the community are called to earn their living properly.
- B. Idleness is not a Christian way to live.
- C. Each person must use the talents in which they have been trained.
- D. This is the way to prepare for the Parousia.

    II.   Christians today are called to honor God with their work.
- A. Idleness is never a Christian value.
- B. God calls each person to use the talents they have been given.
- C. The Parousia will come on its own, but we participate in its coming by living responsibly in hopefulness.

Plan C

Focus: The Day of the Lord will come like a thief in the night (1 Thess 5:2).

Function: To enable hearers to stay alert to God's plan for our universe

I. A thief in the night:
   A. Wishes to be concealed.
   B. Works quickly.
   C. Is not living properly.
   D. Hurts others.

II. Promise of the Day of the Lord.
   A. The time is concealed.
   B. It will not be harmful to those who stay alert.
   C. Paul encourages Christians to live as children of the light.

III. We do not know the day or the hour.
   A. We, too, must live as children of the light.
   B. Do not look for false peace and security.
   C. Live in faith and love, wearing the helmet as our hope of salvation.

Plan D

Focus: Remain worthy of the call of Christ (2 Thess).

Function: To enable the hearers to live in hope, recognizing the signs of God's coming

I. The writer teaches the community not to be stressed about the Parousia.
   A. God's judgment is fair.
   B. To the upright, God promises the first fruits of salvation.
   C. Christians must resolve to work in faith, accepting God's grace through the Spirit.

II. The writer encourages all to recognize the signs of the return of God.
   A. Look for a time of rebellion due to lawlessness.
   B. Lawlessness is wicked deception.
   C. Hope comes to those who believe that God will snatch the lawless one away.

III. Christians today are also called to upright living and alertness.
   A. Stand firm and hold fast to the tradition.
   B. While they wait, stay away from idleness.
   C. This living will give firm hope and eternal comfort.

As we move to chapter 9, we will look at the apocalyptic passages in the Synoptic Gospels, those Gospels that are similar (Matthew, Mark, Luke). We will discover that the same attitude that permeated Paul's initial letters was also present in the Gospels. That is the path to be trod in the pages that follow.

We are pulled forward into a
future we do not want
Come sooner than we feared
Like terror at the thought of judgment
We are not prepared for this.
                                        —*Patrick Marrin*[1]

Chapter Nine

UNMASKING APOCALYPTIC LITERATURE: SYNOPTIC GOSPELS

Later, after the Pauline apocalyptic material had circulated, the
Holy Spirit inspired writers from within the various communities
of faith to pen the story of Jesus in a particular arrangement of the
life/death/resurrection of Jesus that became known as a "gospel."
It was only when the Romans threatened them with destruction of
the Temple that the community of Mark surfaced a writer who
hurriedly told the story of Jesus and his disciples from this perspective of crisis. The Greek word *euthus*, properly translated
"immediately," sets the quickened tone of the Gospel (see Mark
1:10, 1:12, 1:18, 1:20, 1:23).[2] It is clear that Mark wrote about
Jesus the Suffering Servant in order to help the community
endure persecution as the Messiah did and to ready themselves for
the second coming of Jesus, which had been promised. Mark 13
gives the overall apocalyptic vision of the destruction of evil and
the reason for hope in the final coming of Jesus as Messiah.

As time went on and the Messiah did not return, the Gospels of
Luke and Matthew retell the earlier Markan account from two
different perspectives: that of a completely Gentile community

112

and that of a Jewish-Christian community being threatened by an influx of Gentiles. We discover in Luke 21 and Matthew 24–25 that these apocalyptic passages set a slightly different tone for their communities than the apocalyptic passage of Mark.

THE COMMUNITIES OF THE SYNOPTIC GOSPELS IN CRISIS

Each writer of a Synoptic Gospel lived in a different period of biblical Christianity and, therefore, experienced a different crisis. The first description pertains to Mark, since his Gospel is most likely the first written.

Mark's Gospel was written between 65 and 70 CE from the city of Rome. The community consisted of Jewish Christians from the Diaspora (outside the land of Palestine), along with early Gentile converts to Christianity. Some members of this community had most likely migrated from Palestine and had memories of the Temple in Jerusalem. At the time the Gospel was penned, these members felt frustrated because the Romans threatened to destroy the Temple. Numerous references to the Temple show the immediacy (Greek: *euthus*) of this crisis (see Mark 11:2, 11:3, 11:15, 11:27, 12:35, 13:1). The writer Mark was concerned about these new Christians and wanted them to endure the loss of the Temple without backing out of their faith commitment. So he emphasizes the Suffering Servant paradigm (see Isa 53) as a model of Jesus that the community must embrace.

The Gospels of Luke and Matthew are patterned after Mark. The communities of these authors likely had a copy of Mark and probably used it in their early liturgical services. However, the communities were experiencing different crises, and they needed new Gospel accounts that reflected these new crises of the 80s.

The writer of Luke was undoubtedly a Gentile Christian living in a completely Gentile Christian community. Luke's community was aware that the Temple had been destroyed 10–15 years earlier (see 13:34–35, 19:41–44, and 21:20–24) and that Jesus had not returned as the people expected. Because the community was Gentile, it probably knew only the Septuagint First

Testament (that written in Greek), so it was important for the writer Luke to edit out purely Hebrew terms and geography of Palestine that his community would not know. Instead, Luke focused on the Greek world with a "church" beyond Jerusalem. The crisis for Luke is that of living as a *model* Christian in a pagan Roman Empire.

Luke also thinks it important to tell a bigger story than Mark told, a story that included the birth of Jesus and also the life of the Christian community after the resurrection of Jesus. Luke's two works are the largest contribution of any single author in the entire Second Testament. Today's Christians are indebted to Luke for the life of the early church told in the Acts of the Apostles.

It is unfortunate that the Gospel of John separates Luke's two books in the canonical scriptures. Readers must always think of them together. The two works give readers three time frames in the salvation of God's people. The time of *promise* when Israel prepares to receive the Messiah is presented with a genealogy (Luke 3:23). It covers the time from creation through the ministry of John the Baptist (Luke 1:1–2:52).

The time of *Jesus* tells of the fulfillment of God's promise and begins with the baptism of Jesus and the release of the Holy Spirit upon him. When Jesus goes back to God at the crucifixion, Luke again mentions the power of the Spirit. The time of Jesus ends when disciples experience Ascension and are told both to choose someone to replace Judas and to prepare for God's Spirit to come upon them. This time of Jesus includes the preparation of the Messiah (3:1–4:13), the ministry of Jesus in Galilee (4:14–9:50), the journey to Jerusalem (9:51–19:44), and the suffering and victory of Jesus (19:45–24:53, Acts 1:1–11).

Last, the time of *the church* is recorded in Acts of the Apostles and emphasizes that the ministry of Jesus is continued through the apostles and disciples anointed by the Spirit of God at Pentecost. The Christian community is commissioned by God's Spirit to follow in the path of Jesus, doing what they had seen him do and speaking of God in the way they had been taught.

The writer of Matthew's Gospel, perhaps the tax collector who is also called Levi, leads a community of Jewish Christians who are concerned about integrating the Jewish Law with the gospel learned from Jesus. One of Matthew's key phrases, "It was said of old...but I say to you...," allows the community to study the differences between their new life and their life in Judaism. Besides this crisis of "unlearning in order to learn," Matthew's community also had to deal with an influx of Gentile converts who were not aware of the Jewish Law but desired to learn the new message of Jesus. Matthew's Gospel, then, is built upon the fulfillment of the prophecies of old and the recognition of the laws that must be modified.

THE HOPEFUL WORD OF THE GOSPEL'S APOCALYPTIC CHAPTERS

Since each community crisis described in the previous section was unique, that specific crisis leads the writer to pen a different message in the apocalyptic chapter(s). Beginning with chapter 13 of Mark, this section gives specific information pertaining to these differences.[3] The reader will notice that the basic elements are thoroughly described in Mark's Gospel. Thus, when Luke and Matthew reshape Mark, they do so with respect to the concerns of their unique communities.

Mark

Mark 13 is the only chapter in this Gospel with a lengthy discourse by Jesus. Some commentators have called this chapter the last will and testament of Jesus since it gives a vision of hope to this community experiencing the crisis of the imminent destruction of the Temple in Jerusalem. Understanding chapter 13's extremely organized structure might assist preachers and teachers when they encounter Mark 13 in their specific preparations.

- Mark 13:1–5a   Introduction for the disciples
- Mark 13:5b–23   Present time preliminary to the end time
- Mark 13:24–27   Triumph of the Son of Man
- Mark 13:28–31   End coming soon
- Mark 13:32–37   Watch: Only God knows the exact time

Several themes come to the fore in this thirteenth chapter of Mark, a Gospel that has consistently emphasized the suffering Messiah. The disciples are warned not to be led astray (13:5) by false prophets who identify themselves as the Messiah but come to tell them that suffering is not the way. Beware, Mark says (13:5b). Just as the Messiah suffers, so will the holy ones experience suffering.

By inserting chapter 13 immediately before the passion of Jesus and after the entrance into Jerusalem on a donkey, Mark shows that suffering is central to the coming of the end time. The Markan community might have become discouraged when they heard of the imminent destruction of the Temple. They might have been thinking that God was not concerned about them—as God's presence was so often identified with the Temple. In spite of such thinking, Mark portrays the fact that Jesus choice of suffering emphasizes his divinity. The Son of Man will triumph and thus will give strength to those who endure suffering in the name of Jesus.

Mark gives the disciples a clue as to what needs doing before the end time comes. The clue is that "the good news must first be proclaimed to all nations" (Mark 13:10). So, the apocalyptic vision of the Son of Man "coming in clouds with great power" (13:26) gives the community strength to pay attention to what needs doing and to endure the suffering they will experience because they are following in the path of the Suffering Messiah.

There is a threefold cycle in Mark 13 that reaffirms the threefold prediction of the passion of Jesus in Mark 8–10. That earlier pattern predicted Jesus' death and stressed the fact that the disciples did not yet understand. A teaching on discipleship concluded that pattern (see 8:31, 32–33, 34–38; 9:30–32, 33–34, 35–37; and 10:33–34, 35–41, 42–45). This new threefold cycle magnifies the earlier predictions by emphasizing the power of Jesus, the tribulation of the disciples who stayed with him, even though they didn't understand, and finally, the saving event for these faithful disciples. Table 4 brings this pattern to the fore for teachers and preachers studying this chapter.

Table 4. The Threefold Cycle of Mark 13, Emphasizing Salvation of the Elect

Power	Tribulation	Saving Event
13:5b–6, "Beware that no one leads you astray. Many will come in my name and say, 'I am he!' and they will lead many astray."	13:7–13a, "When you hear of wars and rumors of wars, do not be alarmed; this must take place....Nation will rise against nation....Beware; for they will hand you over to councils....You will be hated by all because of my name."	13:b, "But the one who endures to the end will be saved."
13:14a, "But when you see the desolating sacrilege set up where it ought not to be (let the reader understand)."	13:14b–19, "Those in Judea must flee to the mountains....For in those days there will be suffering...."	13:20b, "But for the sake of the elect, whom he chose, he has cut short those days."
13:21–22, "'Look! Here is the Messiah!'...Do not believe it. False messiahs...will appear...to lead astray, if possible, the elect."	13:24–25, "But in those days, after that suffering, the sun will be darkened...and the powers in the heavens will be shaken."	13:27, "Then [the Son of Man] will send out the angels, and gather his elect from the four winds, from the ends of the earth to the ends of heaven."

An important theology lies within this chapter of Mark's Gospel. Because it was written near the time of the destruction of the Temple, the chapter relates the end times to that event. However, it does not answer the question "when." Instead, it answers the question of "who" has the power to save and what the disciple must do in order to endure the suffering until the time of the triumph of the Son of Man. Mark's community is instructed to follow the example of Jesus, even if it leads to suffering.

Preachers and teachers can translate this message for their particular community of faith. Mark 13 emphasizes the cross as the supreme way to follow Jesus. However, what gives meaning to the cross is the vision of the Son of Man coming on the clouds. God is the agent of the time of fulfillment, and the community is encouraged to live in hope by fully embracing the vision of Jesus in a theology of imagination. When people imagine, then they can achieve the hoped-for reality, and when people dream of the fulfillment of God's vision, then the difficult path they must live will keep them focused on the heavenly realm.

Luke

Luke's community was in a far different place than Mark's. Thus, Luke felt compelled to change Mark's apocalyptic section in subtle ways in order to allow this Gospel to speak more clearly to his Gentile Christian community. Preachers and teachers will be assisted in their use of Luke's apocalyptic chapter if they pay attention to the following differences.

One thing that is immediately noticeable is that Luke's chapter 21, the parallel of Mark 13, begins with the story of the poor widow putting money into the Temple treasury (Luke 21:1–4). Mark had concluded chapter 12 with this same story, but Luke wants to emphasize the modeling of this widow for his Gentile community that will be facing great strife before an undetermined end time.

A second important issue is the general nature of the address concerning the Temple. In Mark, while Jesus speaks to his disciples about the Temple, Luke has *some* speaking about the Temple, with no mention of the original Twelve. In this way, Luke sets a contrast between the widow who is a model and the many who will come in the name of Jesus (Luke 21:8a) who are not models. Jesus says, "The time is at hand! Do not go after them" (Luke 21:8b).

What follows is a reference to the signs that must take place before the end, which "will not follow immediately" (Luke 21:9c). Luke's community is living after the Temple destruction, and so the author does not relate the end times to that event. The author of Luke also notes that the signs "will be terrors and great signs from heaven" (Luke 21:11c).

Chapter 21 continues with a reference to the false prophets laying their hands upon the members of the community and persecuting them (Luke 21:12a). The author wants the community to know that "this will be the time" (Luke 21:13a) for them to bear witness to their belief in Jesus. But they do not need to meditate (pray) about their answer, for Jesus will give them "words and a wisdom that none of [their] adversaries will be able to withstand or contradict" (Luke 21:15). For Luke, the community is always called to model their lives upon Jesus and all followers, both in word and deed and, for some, even in death (Luke 21:16b). Showing his belief in Jesus' resurrection as the continuation of new life, Luke indicates that not a hair of their heads will perish, but their endurance will win them life (Luke 21:18–19).

Luke also clarifies that Jerusalem will be "surrounded by armies" (Luke 21:20) and, instead of the destruction of the Temple, that move by the armies will be the sign that the end is near. However, some in the community (that is, the Gentiles) will be called to the city while some leave it (Luke 21:21). It is very important for Luke's community to realize that "Jerusalem will be trampled on by the Gentiles, until the times of the Gentiles are fulfilled" (Luke 21:24). Luke had predicted that fulfillment in chapter 17, when the lighting up of the skies would indicate the glory of the Son of Man (Luke 17:24).

The Gospel writer also emphasizes the distress of nations at the roaring of the sea and how some might faint with fear (Luke 21:25b–26a). But he makes it clear that those Gentiles who are attuned to modeling Jesus' death leading to life will look up and raise their heads, because their redemption is drawing near (Luke 21:28). These Gentiles will get their strength for this time of trial by watching at all times, but especially by praying that they would have strength to escape these trials in order to stand before the living Son of Man (Luke 21:36). The community had already been warned in chapter 12 to be ready for that "unexpected hour" to come upon them (Luke 12:40).

Last, Luke reminds the community that those who are "weighed down with dissipation and drunkenness and the worries of this life" (Luke 21:34) will find themselves not ready for the new life of the Son of Man. Thus, his final recommendation is that the community "be alert at all times, praying that [they] may have the strength to escape all these things that will take place" (Luke 21:36). Instead of the Markan focus on Jesus as the

Suffering Servant, the Lukan Jesus will take the community through death into new life.

Matthew

Although following Mark quite closely, Matthew's first apocalyptic section—chapter 24—makes some important changes that are unique to this Jewish writer. Preachers and teachers will enrich their sermons and classes on Matthew by paying close attention to these changes.

First, readers will notice that the four disciples named by Mark become the disciples in Matthew (Matt 24:3), perhaps indirectly emphasizing the Twelve instead of the four. This would be important for Matthew's community, which follows the pattern of the Twelve Tribes of Israel. Another initial difference is the use of the title "the Christ" (Matt 24:5), which in Greek is literally "the Anointed One" but in Hebrew and Aramaic is "the Messiah."[4] Matthew stresses that Jesus is the promised one for whom the Jewish Christians had been waiting.

Matthew speaks of the many false prophets who will arise (Matt 24:11) and will try to lead the Twelve astray. If that happens, the false prophets will deliver them up to tribulation, and put them to death (Matt 24:9a). Matthew 10 then parallels Mark 13:9–13 with two significant differences:

1. The disciples are to bear witness before the governors and kings "and the Gentiles" (Matt 10:18b), opening the community to Gentiles who will be taught by Jewish Christians.
2. Matthew adds to the [Holy] Spirit of Mark the phrase "of your Father" (Matt 10:20), implying a complexity to God for which the early writer had no other words.

Then, moving back to Matthew 24, the writer adds significantly to Mark 13:9–13. The disciples will be hated "by all nations," which is likely how the Matthean Jews felt. Matthew emphasizes the results of such hatred when he says, "Many will fall away and betray one another...and many false prophets will arise and lead many astray. And because wickedness is multiplied, most [Jewish disciples'] love will grow cold" (Matt 24:10–12). The writer of

Matthew 24 concludes this section with an emphatic statement about what must happen before the end: "This good news of the kingdom will be proclaimed throughout the world, as a testimony to all the nations; and then the end will come" (Matt 24:14).

Matthew continues to emphasize prophecies from the First Testament by saying that the desolating sacrilege was "spoken of by the prophet Daniel" (Matt 24:15), which speaks to his Jewish community that the Christ is truly the Messiah promised in the words of old. Also, in that section of the text, Matthew slips in "or on the Sabbath" to the flight that might have to happen in wintertime. The community is to pray that this will not happen, for it would desecrate the Sabbath.

Matthew also adds significantly to what has been told them beforehand (Mark 13:21–23). They are told not to go out in the wilderness (that is, the desert) to find the Messiah. They are not to believe that he is in the inner rooms (possibly a reference to the inner sanctum of the Temple). Instead, the Son of Man will come in the way nature works, just as "the lightning comes from the east and flashes as far as the west" (Matt 24:26–27).

Matthew concludes chapter 24 in two important ways. He adds an important phrase in verses 29–31: When the Son of Man appears in heaven, "all the tribes of the earth will mourn" (which, undoubtedly, refers to the Twelve Tribes of Israel). Is it because Matthew's community has not accepted all the tribes and, thus, is not ready for the Son of Man to come? Perhaps this added phrase is calling Matthew's community to more inclusiveness.

Second, where Mark sketches the parable of the servants put in charge of a man's property (Mark 13:33–37), Matthew draws out that same parable in chapter 25. In chapter 24, however, Matthew speaks about not knowing when "your Lord is coming" (Matt 24:42) and stresses the theme of watchfulness by telling about the householder not knowing when the thief was coming. That householder does not save his property, but the faithful and wise servant, who knows when his master is coming, will be put over the master's many possessions. Matthew's point, akin to Luke's, is that some in his community are hypocrites by not being watchful but by drinking with the drunken and beating the wicked servants (Matt 24:49).

Matthew adds a second apocalyptic chapter with these three parables: of the ten virgins, of the waste of talents, and of the judgment of the nations. Luke and Mark have pieces of these parables, but in significantly different places. Luke 12:35–38 stresses the goodness of the ones who keep their lamps burning, and Luke 19:11–27 gives his account of the parable of the talents. On the other hand, Mark 13:33–37 emphasizes watchfulness, for one does not know the day nor the hour, and also speaks of a man on a journey who puts his servants in charge to be watchful. Matthew alone has the parable of the judgment of the nations.

By grouping these three parables together into an apocalyptic conclusion that begins with a very important "then," Matthew tells the parables as if he hopes that this is what will happen at the Parousia. George Montague points out that the wedding feast is unlike any Middle Eastern practice. Thus, most scholars would view this first parable, an allegory of the reign of God, as a wedding feast (see Matt 22:1–14 and Rev 19:9) or Jesus as the bridegroom (Matt 9:15) or the church as the bride (Rev 21:2, 9, 17, and Eph 5:25–26).[5] Matthew tells his community that they only have one chance to relearn what they might not have learned previously. They must take their oil with them, that is, they must do good works the first time and every time.

The parable of the talents is cautioning the leaders of Matthew's community, who have received more, that they must use what they have been given wisely. However, he also speaks to others in the community that their reception of divine gifts must be cherished and used, not wasted. The fact that the master is gone *a long time* indicates that, for Matthew's community, the coming of the Son of Man is not to be expected immediately. Even though this is what Matthew taught, he also stresses that the third servant has acted with fear that paralyzes him. He knows that the master expects more, but he is unable to deliver because of his immobility. According to Matthew, this servant ends in tragedy, being thrown into the outer darkness, the place of the damned.

Matthew draws this picture of judgment to an end with the parable of all the nations, the most final, universal, and climactic conclusion to the public ministry of Jesus. In this parable, judgment is not based upon titles or roles, but upon deeds. *Come*, calls the elect of Matthew's community, to reap the promises of living as they learned in the Sermon on the Mount (Matt 5–7). George Montague expresses the power of this parable as a call to holiness. Holiness is neither words nor geographical nor genetic closeness to Jesus; it is neither titles nor external show of piety. Instead, holiness is *doing* the will of the merciful Father, which is love in action.

This might be a very harsh ending for apocalyptic hope to be relished. Nevertheless, it calls Christians to bear the name of Jesus with the same dignity with which Jesus lived and died. According to Matthew, Christians have been given a superabundance of gifts, and the author hopes that they will use them for service to all humankind.

Preaching and Teaching Hope from the Gospel Apocalyptic Chapters

Once again, preaching plans are given as assistance to those who are called to preach from the apocalyptic texts of the Synoptic Gospels. They may also be used to assist in planning lectures for classes. These apocalyptic texts are used as readings on several Sundays in the various lectionaries (see the Appendix). They may also be chosen as readings during times of crisis. Again, I remind preachers that the plans include focus and function statements and a basic structural outline but must be modified by using personal and congregational stories.

Plan A

Focus: Jesus gives a vision of hope as his last will and testament to those experiencing the destruction of the Temple (Mark).

Function: To enable hearers to find hope in the midst of suffering

    I.   The purpose of a last will and testament:
       A. To give perspective to hearer's lives.
       B. To lift the spirits of those who are feeling the loss of a loved one.

C. To leave loved ones with a gift of courage amid suffering.

II. The meaning of the destruction of the Temple for Mark's community.

    A. God was most present in the Temple's inner sanctuary.

    B. Could God be found elsewhere?

    C. Had God promised to return at the destruction of the Temple?

III. A last will and testament at the Temple's destruction for Mark's Gospel hearers today.

    A. The perspective is one of finding hope, even though God might seem absent.

    B. Hearts are lifted by the spirit in the promised return of Jesus.

    C. Courage is found amid suffering when there is hope that God will always be present in one's life.

Plan B

Focus: Do not be led by false prophets (Mark).

Function: To enable hearers to walk the narrow path without interference

I. False prophets were present in the Christian disciples' lives.

    A. These false prophets identified themselves as the Messiah.

    B. They told the Markan Christian community that they could bypass suffering.

    C. Mark says, Beware!

II. The narrow path includes suffering for those in Mark's community.

    A. Mark places his apocalyptic message first, before the Passion account.

    B. Mark's Christians are to carry the cross in the place of Jesus.

    C. For Mark, suffering is central to the end times.

   III. Christians today can learn from Mark's community.

       A. There are false prophets who preach and teach Christianity without suffering in our day.

       B. Christians can be led astray by these false prophets.

       C. Mark encourages today's Christians to embrace the cross.

       D. By doing that, they also embrace those who have the cross thrust upon them by life circumstances.

Plan C

Focus: Watch; only God knows the exact time or day (Mark/Luke/Matthew).

Function for Mark: To enable hearers to continue to preach or teach the good news until the end

    I. Mark's disciples were preoccupied.

       A. They are not to be bothered by "when."

       B. They are to be concerned only with "what needs doing."

    II. Only God knows the exact time.

       A. The community must be as watchful as a thief in the night.

       B. They will be watchful in hope and have strength to endure.

       C. For the Son of Man comes on the clouds.

       D. Do these Christians know how to imagine that?

   III. Today's Markan Christians must also be watchful.

       A. They do not know the day nor the hour.

       B. They, too, must be as watchful as a thief in the night.

       C. They must pay attention to what needs doing.

       D. Can they be hopeful by imagining that time of glory?

Function for Luke: To enable hearers to model their lives after Jesus until the end

I.   Luke's disciples are to model themselves after the poor widow.
   A.   She gave all she had to God.
   B.   She did so with humility.
   C.   This is what Lukan disciples are to learn about Jesus through this widow.

II. Many others will come in the name of Jesus.
   A.   Disciples must be watchful that they are not following the false prophets.
   B.   Disciples are to bear witness to Jesus by the way they live and by what they say.
   C.   Even death cannot take them away from life.

III. Today's Lukan Christians must also be models in watchfulness and prayer.
   A.   Prayer leads to hope, which assists us through death to new life.
   B.   True disciples today will be models in total giving and humility.
   C.   We disciples of Jesus are not to be led astray by false prophets.
   D.   We disciples must pray that we can keep our eyes fixed on the glory of Jesus.

Function for Matthew: To enable hearers to become wise and faithful servants

I.   The householders are not ready.
   A.   They allowed their property to be trampled upon.
   B.   They did not take care of the master's property.
   C.   They are hypocritical because they get drunk and beat their servants.

II. Wise and faithful servants are ready.
   A.   They take great care of the master's many possessions.
   B.   They are not hypocrites, but live life in the name of Jesus.
   C.   They are as watchful for God's glory as they are of the master's possessions.

    III. Today's Matthean Christians are called to be watch-
ful as well.

      A. We are not to be like the hypocritical house
holder.

      B. We are to care for our master's many possessions
with integrity.

      C. We are to be wise and faithful servants.

      D. Then, we too, will have the hopeful imagination
to see God's glory.

Plan D

Focus: When the Son of Man appears, all the tribes of the
earth will mourn (Matthew).

Function: To enable hearers to be inclusive of all peoples of the
earth

    I. The Twelve Tribes represent all peoples of the earth.

      A. For Matthew's Jewish Christians, acceptance of
the Gentiles was essential.

      B. God came to save all people and so the tribes do
not need to mourn.

      C. These Jewish Christians must enlarge their con-
cept of God's salvation.

    II. Today's Matthean Christians are also called to inclu-
siveness.

      A. Inclusiveness today must be enlarged to receive
all religions and cultures.

      B. The tribes will still mourn if Christians close the
door to others.

      C. Christians' concept of God must always be
stretched.

      D. God wishes to save all humanity and the
Christian's concept must include that reality.

Plan E

Focus: At the time of the Parousia, Matthean Christians are
called to holiness (Matthew).

Function: To enable hearers to know what holiness entails

    I.   The reign of God is like a wedding feast.
- A. Matthew warns his community to have their oil lamps ready.
- B. Have they learned to do good works consistently?

    II.   The reign of God is like those who use their talents fully.
- A. Matthew says to leaders, The more you have, the more is expected of you.
- B. Matthew says to all that gifts (talents) must be used, not wasted.
- C. Matthew says to those who tend to bury their talents not to act with paralyzing fear.

    III.   The reign of God is like those who do the will of God.
- A. For Matthew, holiness is more than a show of piety.
- B. For Matthew, holiness is more than "closeness" to Jesus.
- C. For Matthew, holiness is following the Sermon on the Mount.

    IV.   Today's Matthean Christians are also called to holiness.
- A. How is our oil of "good works" made ready?
- B. How are our talents being used fully?
- C. How have we done the will of God in the way we live?
- D. These are critical questions to move us toward the reign of God.

The last part of our investigation of the apocalyptic passages in the Second Testament is the crowning jewel of all the apocalyptic material in the entire Bible. Chapter 10 unmasks the Book of Revelation as the book that brings us full circle—from God's revelation to an initial couple in the Garden of Eden to God's revelation through a writer named John to the seven churches of Asia Minor.

Darkness is not all,
Nor war the last word;
not by a long shot, or a short.
The children speak it;
the last word. Hope.
Hope; the children.
The child.

—*Yehuda Amicai*[1]

Chapter Ten

UNMASKING APOCALYPTIC LITERATURE: BOOK OF REVELATION

At a much later period, a writer named John presents an imaginary picture book of the destruction of all evil and the reign of God in glory. The Book of Revelation, the only apocalypse in the Bible, is the pinnacle of apocalyptic material in the Second Testament. An entire commentary would be needed to give all details of this book. The overview presented in this chapter gives details about its most significant themes.

JOHN'S COMMUNITY IN CRISIS

The most obvious way it is known that crisis exists for John and the seven churches is that the author indicates that he shares with the seven churches "the persecution...and the patient endurance" (1:9). What was the persecution he was sharing with them? And what did they have to endure patiently?

Most commentators would agree that there was some type of persecution of Christians going on in the Roman Empire during the reign of Emperor Domitian as well as the reign of Trajan, who followed Domitian. The major complaint against Christians was their refusal to participate in emperor worship at the various temples constructed to the "Emperor god." This refusal meant that they held to their belief in one God, thereby identifying themselves as Christians.

Regular correspondence between Pliny, the governor of Bithynia in northern Asia Minor, and Trajan, the emperor, has been preserved that speak of the trials of Christians and the penalties imposed upon them. There seems to be no way out for these Christians, because if they admit they are Christian, they are given a second chance to deny it. If they deny their identity as Christian, then they are given an opportunity to participate in emperor worship at the temple enshrined to the emperor's power. This way they would stay in good graces with the emperor while, at the same time, admitting that the emperor was greater than their God. However, if they admit their Christianity a second time, they are then sentenced to death.

It is unclear whether these seven churches in Asia Minor were experiencing such persecution. Perhaps they were not subjected to persecution at the time that John wrote these letters. Nevertheless, even if there is no persecution at that time in that specific place, Christians of the 90s still heard of persecution in the empire. Because of that, they likely feared the possibility of persecution in the near future, and often such psychological persecution can be more upsetting than the persecution itself.

So, John writes his visions to these churches in order to support them during the difficult days they were experiencing. The author hopes that these Christian communities might face their own betrayals or neglect of the one God and find hope in his visions that God would, indeed, destroy all evil. John wants them to see the bigger picture of the final judgment against evil and the invitation of the faithful to God's banquet in the eternal Jerusalem.

HOPEFUL WORDS OF THE BOOK OF REVELATION

As we continue to live within this new millennium, the Book of Revelation requires careful study.[2] Many Christians want to use this book as a guide for what they believe is a critical time in history before the end time is inaugurated. Because of the book's length, it is impossible to do a thorough summary of every chapter of Revelation. Therefore, the hopeful words presented here come from an investigation of four major themes that emerge from the Book of Revelation:

1. That Jesus Christ, victorious over evil, now rules the entire universe (Rev 1:18–19)
2. That a struggle exists between the desire for power and the implementation of justice (Rev 18)
3. That people can decide for Jesus and against oppressive power (Rev 2–3)
4. That there is a future for God's people that will come with Christ's victory (Rev 20)

Notice that these major themes are gleaned from Revelation 1 to 3 and 18 to 20. These chapters form the heart of the essential message that encompasses the Book of Revelation. The other chapters, which show the various ways that *good wins over evil*, must be studied in depth from other commentaries.[3] Preachers and teachers might be assisted in some of their preparation of the Book of Revelation if they pay attention to these themes.

Christ Rules

The first theme concerns Jesus' salvific role. Jesus, the Lamb slain (Rev 5:6), has been made worthy (4:11). This reverses the tragedy of the crucifixion, for Jesus as Christ now rules with God (3:21). John was convinced that the final age had begun when Jesus took upon himself the evil of the world and, victorious over it, became the only source of salvation. Of course, we know that the final age is still coming, two thousand-plus years later. As

Mark poignantly indicates, only God knows the day and the hour (Mark 13:32). It is for us to live in hope with our faces turned toward good and away from evil.

Revelation helps people recognize evil in the world and in their life, and celebrates God's final victory over it. The book presents the conflict between good and evil in several different ways. Gone is the legitimate submission to Roman authority that Paul counsels (Rom 13:1–7). Evil's enormity is envisioned with the harlot seated upon the scarlet throne (Rev 17:1–6), the beast rising out of the sea (13:1–4), and the dragon temporarily bound (20:7–10). This evil is rejected by the absolute victory of Jesus. Babylon, the symbol of evil Rome in Revelation, is destroyed.

John, then, expresses the hope for the enthronement of Christ. It is this Christ who saves faithful Christians. He is present in the midst of the seven churches (see Rev 2:1–3 :22). According to John, these Christians are witnessing the birth pangs of the final era of salvation and must continue their fight against evil to the end.

Many values are at odds with Christian living today as well— sexism, racism, consumerism, militarism, the disregard for human life and the poor. Christians will profit from a book that speaks sharply of the conflict between good and evil. Because it is so easy to become blind to the evil around us, Christians need to ask where—in the world atlases of their own lives—Babylon has again made its home. Preachers and teachers can assist Christians in their belief that Christ crucified still reigns, giving hope against every Babylon.

Power and Justice

The second theme concerns the struggle between desire for power and implementation of justice. The central theological question of Revelation is the question of power: *To whom does the earth belong?* Christians of John's day felt powerless when they came into conflict with Rome, though they were convinced that power belonged with Jesus alone.

Revelation 18 describes the final destruction of political power. The center of antagonism against Christian faith collapses in a great dirge: "Fallen, fallen is Babylon the great" (18:2). The visionary does not consider how believers are to live within the state. Instead, he portrays the collapse of a monstrous power trying to defeat the purpose of God. Chapter 18 has three units. The first describes the fall of Babylon (18:1–3), the second gives the reaction of its residents (18:4–20), while the final unit describes the destruction with an angel throwing a huge millstone into the sea (18:21–24). This picture of absolute desolation concludes with wild beasts inhabiting the city and howling creatures dancing among its ruins.

God's people emerge from this hostile city, rejoicing with musical instruments. The punishment of those who are left is in proportion to their once luxurious life. For example, kings and merchants chant dirges that usually express mourning (19:9–19), but in their case announces judgment against insincere proclaimers. The city's lights go out as the blood of innocent victims cries for justice.

This description intensifies the injustice in the empire. The Talmud implies that ten measures of wealth came down into the world: Rome received nine, and others in the world one. The Roman Empire has secured power by crushing the oppressed. So, John encourages Christians by telling them how the power of the world competes with God who is rebuilding a just world as an unjust world passes away.

This is an important message for today. When oppression is caused by social conditions or by excesses within political or religious authority, the Book of Revelation will force Christians to question that exercise of power. Struggles that evoke such tension include:

- Struggles between nations: arms race, lust for power
- Struggles within society: self-indulgence, crime, and political and economic corruption
- Struggles within the church: denial of sexual sins among leadership, non-inclusiveness in order to retain certain structures, and overconcern for the church's survival
- Struggles on the personal level: compromising truth and ethical behavior to get ahead

Believers, aware of unjust use of power, often face a crisis of faith. They need teachers and preachers who will help them move toward trust in God alone, which will give believers courage to identify injustice and to replace unjust power with the loving hands of God.

Resisting Evil

The third theme emphasizes the ability of people to decide for Jesus and against the power structures. The author encouraged the faithful to resist evil, no matter what the consequences. John knew that good and evil are personal as well as collective, so people cannot remain neutral. The author wanted them to act upon their faith convictions, putting their lives on the line against these power structures.

John defended Jesus' claim as the world's ruler by asking his Christian readers, *To whom do you belong, to whom do you give your power, and for what do you live, even in the face of death?* This questioning taught Christians to have faith in the face of persecution. The mistreatment they experienced emptied them of their own insecurities and opened them to complete dependence upon God. Writing to each church (2:1–3:22), John had them look within and without for enemies that would keep them away from God. This prepared them for the final judgment, the culmination of each person's choices. Along with the fall of Babylon (18–19), these letters helped Christians deal with feelings of fear and revenge by overcoming tension between what existed and what was desired. They learned that Christianity could not survive without the purification of persecution. Jesus achieved victory only in death. Could his followers expect anything less?

Those who help Christians decide for Jesus is essential today as well. Preachers and teachers might wish to speak about the seven churches addressed in the Book of Revelation, helping Christians in this decision. These were congregations of real people loved by Christ in the midst of struggle and sometimes evil. It is sad when Christian educators, preachers, and spiritual directors ignore the Book of Revelation because of fear that they do not know its message. Many today need the consoling message of this book, that eventually *good will win over evil*. Others, who might have experienced little oppression, could be challenged by its contents to reach out to those who have nothing.

I suggest that both individuals and the church as a whole use Revelation for reflection and that preachers and teachers use its serious questions to build their reflections. Individual believers might respond in significant ways, some of which include:

- Facing pain and suffering by remembering Jesus' dependence upon a merciful God who assures victory
- Refusing to play the double game of attachment to life, privileges, and comfort while professing faith in Christ and ignoring those who are barely surviving
- Examining one's ability to love, be faithful, stand with truth, fight against evil, be spiritual, be an evangelizer, and have a burning zeal for life
- Developing Christian responses to issues that pit politics against religion, life against death, love against hate, and friendship against vengeance
- Living that victory that belongs to God alone

Preachers and teachers must also pay close attention to the issues the Book of Revelation provides for church leaders. Among others that could be posed are the following:

- Seeking critically its role in the world
- Examining its hesitance to proclaim that God alone establishes true peace
- Teaching baptism as entrance into Christ's death to share his resurrection
- Teaching faith as a letting go of self-sufficiency
- Including in its outlook the prospect of persecution and not being scandalized when it occurs, because witnesses of Christ live a countercultural stance
- Realizing that programs alone do not meet the challenges posed by the realities of our own day

Revelation posed to its seven churches this question: "Will your church survive?" This ought to be a vital question for our churches as well, as we constantly repeat the process of Christ's death and resurrection. Churches must witness to love and justice, even to the point of death. Thus, Revelation can be both a source of hope and a basis for Christian liberation. Whatever our experience now, this book can help people decide for the reign of God.

God's Future

The fourth theme of Revelation is that there is a future for God's people—and a theology of the future is present within the Book of Revelation. The book indicates how the world is being used to unfold the mystery of God. John teaches that people can be a part of the purpose of God or they can resist it, but they cannot separate themselves from it.

Unlike what many might say, the book is not about forecasting the future of the church in minute detail. John shows the people of his time the events of their day as part of a sequence that finishes in Christ's victory. He gave people hope by asserting that their lives had meaning because of their faith in the future.

In the same way, if Revelation speaks of today, it is only because it gives meaning to the lives of believers today. The challenge for Christians now, as then, is to trust that their relationship with God will bring to perfection what began with creation and redemption.

In four steps, Revelation 20 describes the completion of God's purpose:

1. The dragon is chained for a preparation period, negating its influence so the nations are not deceived (20:1–3).
2. The faithful, those who resisted the temptation, return to life during this preparation period (20:4–6).
3. Satan is released again, showing that the human tendency to rebel against the Creator is difficult to overcome—God, however, defeats Satan decisively (20:7–10).
4. Christ returns to execute universal judgment (20:11–15).

Aptly called a theology of hope, the Book of Revelation assures believers that the future will be completely different from the present time of suffering and death. This is a most appropriate message to be used by teachers and preachers for people who feel they belong to a generation without hope. John's belief that hope has no limits is one of victory over seemingly overwhelming odds. The Book of Revelation implies that the question of meaning is never decisively answered in this world. It finds hope in the world to come where "there will be no night" (Rev 21:25).

PREACHING AND TEACHING HOPE FROM THE BOOK OF REVELATION

In the next section of this book, preachers and teachers are presented with plans that give them assistance for working with this apocalyptic Book of Revelation. Passages from Revelation are used as liturgical texts on some Sundays (see the Appendix). They may also be chosen as readings during times of crisis. These plans follow the same format as those presented in previous chapters, with one plan given for each of the four themes presented.

Plan A

Focus: In hope, Christians will turn their faces toward good.

Function: To enable hearers to maintain hope in the midst of evil

    I.   John helped the communities recognize evil.
       A. Submission to authority is only legitimate when not oppressive.
       B. The oppressive Roman government was described as the harlot upon the throne.
       C. Such evil must be rejected as Babylon.

    II. John helped the communities embrace goodness.
       A. Christ sits on the only throne that matters.
       B. Christ is also present in the midst of the seven churches.

    III. Today's Christians must also recognize evil, so they can embrace the good.
       A. It is so easy to become blind to sin.

B. Sin is recognized when named: sexism, racism, militarism....

C. In the end, God's grace will turn Christian faces from evil if they are open.

D. This will give them hope and vision.

Plan B

Focus: Power corrupts justice without a hopeful vision of God.

Function: To enable hearers to become justice seekers in a world of injustice

    I.   The community recognizes the injustices of the political system.

        A. Ten measures to Rome; one measure to all others.

        B. The power of the world cannot continue competing with God.

        C. The city is absolutely desolate with howling creatures dancing among the ruins.

    II. John helped his communities believe that the political power would fall.

        A. The monstrous power falls before God's purpose.

        B. Their punishment is in proportion to their luxurious life.

        C. They cry out in an insincere dirge.

    III. Today's Christians must recognize the injustices in their own society.

        A. Four levels of injustices exist: between nations, within society, within church, and within personal lives.

        B. Believers must face these injustices, even if it leads to a crisis of faith.

        C. They must replace the injustice they see with the love of God.

        D. Then there is hope that God will rule.

Plan C

Focus: People have the ability to decide for Jesus and against the empire.

Function: To enable hearers to decide with integrity of soul

    I.   John saw that decision making could be personally controlled or God controlled.
        A. John pointed out the danger of self-centered decision making.
        B. He showed that the communities became trapped, especially during times of crisis.
        C. But he wanted them to realize that insecurity could lead one to God.

   II.   John's challenge was, "To whom do you belong?"
        A. John forced people to look within themselves and within their communities.
        B. Once they recognized their own evils, they could look without for evil and allow God's Spirit to help them overcome that evil.
        C. The communities trusted that they belonged to God.
        D. They just needed to name that fact.

  III.   Today's Christians must also decide, even if their decision for Christ leads to persecution.
        A. In today's society, it is so easy to be self-sufficient.
        B. Such "go-it-alone-ness" can mask the evil around us.
        C. Let go and let God is not easy, but it is still possible.
        D. God will lead Christians in hope if they allow it.
        E. Preachers and teachers must ask serious questions in the way that John did.

Plan D

Focus: The people of God live with a vision of hope and a future.

Function: To enable the hearers to embrace that vision and that future

I. John teaches that people can be a part of the purpose of God or they can resist it.
   A. It is impossible for people to separate themselves from God.
   B. That is the way of God who loves and is always compassionate.
   C. The events of their day are unfolded before them.
   D. John makes sure they see that it culminates in Christ's victory.

II. Revelation speaks to today's Christians in the same way.
   A. It gives meaning to the lives of believers.
   B. It does not completely present them with the future.
   C. That is part of the mystery of God.
   D. Hope has no limits and leads to victory over seemingly overwhelming odds.

CONCLUSION

In the previous three chapters, we have walked a journey from the letters to the Thessalonians to the Book of Revelation. It has been a journey of hope. God has been made present through the scriptures written so long ago. God's plan continues to unfold. That plan is often revealed through people's imaginations, which can be as active as they wish them to be. Often, however, the dreams have been couched in fantastic drama that may have caused fear, unless people understand the process of imaginings. They do not want their dreams to lead to paralysis, so they must be reminded over and over again of the place of drama in these texts. The time of Advent is a time of the greatest drama, as God reached down on the face of the earth and touched humankind with godly human flesh. Apocalyptic in Advent is an equation that we must understand. It is to that connection that we now turn.

The real voyage of discovery
consists not in seeking
new landscapes
but in having
new eyes.

—Marcel Proust[1]

Chapter Eleven

MOVING TOWARD CHRISTIAN ACTION WITH HOPE

While investigating the apocalyptic texts of the scriptures, it was discovered that amidst the wars, famines, earthquakes, and other ways that apocalyptic writers used to imagine evil's destruction, a thread of hope continued to emerge for the covenant people. From both the Israelite and the Christian perspectives, that hope can be summarized in the simple sentence: *God will ultimately triumph over all evil.*

The crisis element of apocalyptic literature led to Aristotle's definition of tragedy. Apocalyptic literature could not be studied without looking at the crises of history that brought forth writers who, as Aristotle noted, could believe in a God who, in the end, would show how the tragedy concluded. That writer used imagination from the memory of the past along with hope-filled belief in order to write about a future that God has planned for the faithful. The Spirit of God who always promised the covenant people a messiah, the son of man as they named that messiah, inspired these writers' imaginations.

To seize this hope, the tool needed for writers, and ultimately for teachers and preachers, is imagination, which assists one to approach these texts creatively. Their symbols and images were specifically designed to magnify the destructiveness of evil and to glorify the presence of a God who will not stand by while the faithful ones are overwhelmed by evil. Although every person has imagination, often it is underdeveloped and undercultivated. Preachers and teachers of apocalyptic literature ought to revitalize lagging imaginations in order to vibrantly encounter these texts. Preachers and teachers will do that best if they continually develop their own spiritualities (see Table 3 in chapter 5).

From the work of Richard Schechner, a crisis model was introduced in chapter 5 and used to investigate the essential elements of crisis (see Figure 2). Since everyone must deal with crisis at some point in their lives, applying this model to understand crisis in general opened the door to discovering the most vital message of apocalyptic literature: God is in charge. As shown previously, that model could be applied to apocalyptic literature in general and specifically to the preacher or teacher of apocalyptic literature and to the listening community. These elements of the liturgical event, as part of the drama that assists in locating new directions in time of crisis, need to be considered.

Hope was identified in chapter 2 as the requisite virtue of every crisis. Developing an apocalyptic mentality helped people move from crisis with hope. But hope, as virtue, needed to be understood much more clearly. Saint Thomas Aquinas's definition of hope was tied to passion and knowledge of a future good that is hard to obtain. He also categorized the causes and effects of hope and clarified the opposite of hope—despair. Aquinas insisted that hope lead to action, working toward a realistic goal, even a goal beyond one's reach. The highest form of hope for Aquinas was identified as the supernatural virtue, which presupposed that the grace of God in one's life contained incredible magnetism and could inspire both resoluteness and zeal for good.

Also in chapter 2, we saw that Jürgen Moltmann added another important dimension by setting hope within the context of eschatology. He saw a flaw in previous interpretations, where one hoped only for a good not attainable in this life. Thus, hope was not an everyday reality. Countering that notion, Moltmann presented hope as the foundation of theological thinking. He saw that if humans tried to shield themselves from crises, they would soon despair. Moltmann called people toward a believing hope, teaching them to love the entire created universe. His theology allowed for thinking in cosmological terms, while still setting one's feet firmly on the ground. That is exactly what the apocalyptic process was designed to do: to convert humanity as they live in this world and attend to the entire cosmos at the same time.

Theologian Michael Downey and political scientist Glenn Tinder (see chapter 2) contributed to the discussion by reflecting on hope in the postmodern era. Both lamented the pervasive loss of hope, especially among young people, and argued for a reliable and coherent worldview that would lead one to the fullness of hope—that is, to God. Finally, liturgist Richard Fragomeni added that hope meant being surprised by God in order to become fully human and alive.

Concluding with a list of hope's characteristics, these reflections were intended as a tool for preachers and teachers to use while preparing sermons or lectures on apocalyptic texts, especially during times of crisis. The reflections were also connected to First Testament hope, which was aligned with God's promise of fidelity to a specific group of people. The Exodus journey was remembered as the apex of the story of God's promise, with all biblical literature looking both forward and backward upon that story.

INCREASING APOCALYPTIC HOPE

The lectionary readings before the end of the church year encourage living with an apocalyptic mindset, that is, of hope in the midst of crisis. Churches that are not lectionary-based are encouraged to follow the guidelines of chapters 6 through 10 of this volume to choose apocalyptic texts for preaching and teaching at specific times throughout the church year, but especially prior to Christmas.

Since the people who penned the Second Testament lived in the expectation of the second coming of the Messiah, those who identify the Second Testament as their word of God are encouraged to always live with an apocalyptic-like mentality. If that happens, then the path of the Jewish people, still looking for a messiah, and the Muslim people who accept Jesus as a great prophet will join that of Christians, all journeying together toward the Parousia.

Teachers, preachers, and readers must remember that the key to understanding apocalyptic texts is developing a dramatic imagination of a God who always moves before and consoles the people. The same apocalyptic literature that assisted the Jewish and Christian people of old to recognize evil both within and around them will keep them on the path assisting in the destruction of evil. The literature will constantly remind all of God's covenant people that God is definitely in charge of the world and all its creation.

Since the crisis of 9/11, that message can again be a source of hope. Many might still feel a vague anxiety, an edgy fearfulness, and gnawing uncertainty about their own security. Crises often evoke these emotions. However, God's Spirit gives the grace to endure the cosmic struggle on earth between good and evil. Evil exists amid tragedies, but free will cooperates with God's grace. By growing in hope amid crisis, people can develop and live with an apocalyptic mindset. Will they choose hope over despair today?

That is not as easy a task as it may sound. People need to decide what actions bring the human community closer to God's justice and peace. They need to reaffirm their hope that God is in charge. On earth, this freedom to choose will never be cheap grace. Yes, God gives freedom, but humans decide how to cooperate with divine grace, moving toward that day when all evil will be destroyed. Humanity waits for that day when the wolf will lie down with the lamb. It is that hope-filled vision of Isaiah (11:1–9) that forms the core theme of the readings at the end of the liturgical year. The vision, even though tested by crisis, actively guides humanity toward the peace and justice that will allow all God's people to live "on that holy mountain." The holy mountain is symbolic of Zion, where God's people will gather at the end of time. It is used many times in the First Testament, and is important for meditation (see Ps 99:9; Ezek 20:40; Joel 3:17; Dan 9:16, 11:45; and Zech 8:3).

THE TASK OF THE HOPE-FILLED FAITH COMMUNITY

Apocalyptic hope remains a serious concern for the contemporary faith community,[2] committed to answer for the hope that is in it. The author of 1 Peter indicates the importance of hope with the following phrase: "Always be ready to make your defense to anyone who demands from you an accounting for the hope that is in you" (1 Pet 3:15).

If the faith community is to carry the promise of hope to the world today, it is urged to always emphasize God as a promise of hope. Restricting hope to the Advent season alone will not bring us closer to God. Retired Cardinal Archbishop Paulo Evaristo Arns, in an article appropriately titled "From Hope to Hope," clearly indicates the difficulty of hope: "Faith is a gift of God. Love sprouts from our hearts as we see the needs of others. But life is so full of contradictions that it is difficult to have hope and to grow in hope. Humanly speaking, there are moments in our lives when it is almost impossible to hope."[3] Thus, the faith community must work at hoping all year. According to Moltmann, if the faith community fails to do this today, then it lives in denial of the promises of God. He gives three reasons why people might not believe in the promises of God: (1) God lies, not keeping the promises; (2) God is faithful, so something that came to pass was not the promise of God but the lie of false prophets; and (3) the reason for the withholding of the promise is that humanity has departed from the promise and disobeyed the covenant again and again.[4]

Some might not wish to accept such strong language. Thus, as the pilgrim people of God, always *in via* (on the way), the faith community is required to take up the challenge of fulfilling the promise of God, both individually and communally, throughout the ages. Roman Catholic Christians were encouraged by Vatican Council II to be pilgrim people, people of God always on the way toward God. Other Christians, and indeed, all others in the world are also addressed as follows: "There is but one People of God, which takes its citizens from every race, making them citizens of a kingdom which is of a heavenly and not an earthly nature."[5] As Oscar Romero once said, while preaching a funeral homily (March 14, 1977):

> Let us not forget:
> we are a pilgrim church,
>   subject to misunderstanding,
>   to persecution,
> but a church that walks serene
> because it bears the force of love.[6]

Individually, members of the faith community are called to recognize that hope is the extraordinary matter of which their souls are made. Hope keeps them going when life has lost its meaning or things have gone terribly wrong. The challenge seems always the same: How does a person of faith search for hope in the midst of uncertainty, fear, and death? One way is to develop an eschatological view of a coming God amidst a hopeful and waiting people—a God who will ultimately prevail over evil and death and a people who will reflect God's glory.

Separately, patience is the first task of the faithful one, but not the only task. Ethically, God is never found in merely the private world of the individual but must be sought in a universal public good that furthers the liberation of humankind, the Earth, and indeed the entire cosmos. Faithful ones ought to embrace the future every day as a *new reality*. Otherwise, nothing might change at all. Moltmann calls for this new outlook in the following challenge: "We will only be able to overcome the unfruitful and paralyzing confrontation between personal and cosmic hope, between individual and universal eschatology, if we reject the pietistic path of placing the soul at the center of things and also the secular way of making this world central and, instead, focus upon God's glory."[7]

Independently, faithful people are called out of themselves and into a world of love and hope for a just society. According to theologian M. Douglas Meeks, people can know justice if they tell the stories from the remembered past about their neighbors and themselves. He encourages people to find out the stories, identities, loves, passions, commitments, hates, and fears of their community of faith. Then they will be able to speak about the same justice contained in the law of the Torah. Meeks is further convinced that loving individuals, freed from their own guilt and fear of death, are the most promising advocates of justice.[8] Liberation theologian José Míguez Bonino calls for a feminine image of the "mending of creation" as a way of evoking the fullness of the biblical promise. That image for those who are mended people will "keep on keeping on" when they join with others willing to appeal to the memory that lives toward the future and not just hangs on to past tradition.[9] Finally, black theologian James H. Cone indicates that basic to the black person's struggle for liberation is the idea of God's chosen people, for they are the chosen. The black theologian wants to know what the scriptures have to say to "a man [or woman] who is jobless and cannot get work to support his [her] family because the society is unjust."[10] These questions for the black theologian lead from despair to hope only if they have been internalized to the point where it makes the adherent a new person in the fullest ontological sense.

Communally, the work begins with the preacher or teacher, who energizes the imagination of the community with apocalyptic hope amidst any crisis and encourages that work toward justice and love.[11] The task of preachers and teachers in these apocalyptic-like days is the same task as the prophets and apocalyptic writers of old: to preach and teach that the God promised *today* is also the God who made a covenant of hope with the people of the First Testament. This God will ultimately win over all the evil in this world, including that evil perpetuated by 9/11.

According to Brueggemann, the preacher or teacher first draws God into the question of pain. In that light, the preacher/teacher is the same as the prophet of old, who hoped that the "ache of God could penetrate the numbness of history."[12] For Brueggemann and Joseph Jeter, the language of lament is crucial. Jeter indicates that the genius of the Book of Lamentations is that it recognizes times when there is no substitute for the question, "Is there any pain like my pain?"[13] The apocalyptic teacher or preacher is obliged to cut through the grief and, in a state of vulnerability and openness, identify the evil and death. This needs courage and cannot be done unless preachers and teachers have faced their own suffering, which helps them believe in the power of love beyond death. "Death is the last enemy" to be conquered (1 Cor 15:26). Resurrection from the dead is the enemy of death and of a world that puts up with death.

The task of reading God's promise also belongs to the community of faith, which allows the promise to become eschatological. Breaking the boundaries of the old creation—it would not be a repetition of the beginning—God's promise becomes wider than the first creation could have ever been. This apocalyptic view of life fosters and cherishes values that transcend death and bring forth transcendent life.

As a community, humans are called to stand together and look at life in a more vital way than they have ever done before. They ought to open themselves to mysterious hope and cease trying to master every situation. But people cannot move in the opposite direction either. As Pius XII once said, "Humanity should thank God that they are placed in the middle of such difficult problems so that they can't become mediocre."[14]

As a community, people are called to achieve a balance between the taste of death and optimistic hope. Think of this as a horizontal view, seeing the horizon first but using the same perspective to see everything and everyone else in the world around. Hope encourages the faith community to be a constant disturbance in human society, breaking through the best planning and seeing the neighbor in a brand new way. If one sees the neighbor, then one can encounter that neighbor.

Immediately after 9/11, preachers and teachers might have expected church communities to grow. Since that has not happened, the community needs to ask why. A recent article carried statistics about faith since 9/11. Brian Cool, a Roman Catholic chaplain, was disappointed that church communities have fallen back into life as usual. Economic and political leadership seem to be more important than moral and spiritual leadership. Even though Americans have a sense of self-sufficiency, the article reflected that churches have let people off the hook by not infusing them with a deeper sense of faith—one that will withstand any crisis and be more than just another Sunday service.[15]

The kind of faith vision needed by communities depends upon an eruptive Spirit, totally in control of the community's journey toward God. Perhaps an eruptive Spirit is also one with the ability to laugh. Moltmann suggests that laughter is the medium "between the infinite magnitude of our tasks and the limitations of our strength."[16] That statement seemed to interplay laughter and hope: hope is the abstract virtue and laughter is the specific access into hope.

Infinite possibilities await those with hope-filled justice eyes. Perhaps the best way to view these possibilities is to meditate upon the prophet Micah, who offers hope of living the call to justice with three profound expectations: "What does the Lord require of you but to do justice, and to love kindness, and to walk humbly with your God."[17] Hope is the path—a new creation is the image—and life with God in God's Spirit is the goal.

UNDERSTANDING ADVENT WITH APOCALYPTIC EYES

This work would be incomplete without examining more fully why apocalyptic literature appears in the lectionaries of the liturgical year before the season of Advent as well as the first, and sometimes second, week of Advent. According to liturgist Fritz West, Advent can be pictured as two overlapping ovals of memory, the first centered on the second coming and the second on the first coming (see Figure 3). Thus, the memory of the second coming is highlighted in the Sundays leading up to and including some of Advent. The first coming is emphasized in the last couple of Advent Sundays.[18] I remember once hearing Raymond Brown say that apocalyptic literature is used so that adults take the baby out of Christmas and, instead, think about the future.

In a still broader sense, the Advent season in the three-year lectionary presents the life of Jesus, the Christ, by arranging events from his birth to his return in glory.[19] These overlapping circles are like containers of collective memory that depict the Christmas

Figure 3. Advent Liturgical Cycle

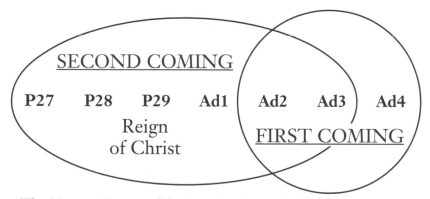

The Memory Pattern of the Last Sundays in Ordinary Time and the
Season of Advent, *Revised Common Lectionary*
Legend: P=Proper; Ad-Advent

cycle as a progression of interlocking geometric shapes. Encased
in the Advent circle are the communal memories of apocalyptic
thought as well as the developing concept of the Messiah. Each of
these circles, however, can be subdivided further. For instance, the
apocalyptic circle could contain three additional circles, each indicating a specific aspect of apocalyptic thought: the cosmic, the
religious, and the personal.

The containers of communal memory for the Christmas season
are the memories of the *logos* (the Word; see John 1:1–18), the
birth of Jesus, and the salvation of Israel. Last, the containers of
communal memory for the season of Epiphany consist of three
interlinking developments: that of the church, the Savior of the
World, and the Son of God.

Apocalyptic thought assists you in picturing the Advent/
Christmas/Epiphany cycle within a much wider context than any
of us regularly think about. In our secular world, with its unbri-
dled consumerism, there is a danger of losing the real meaning of
Christmas. The broader context helps you to visit the crèche with
an expectation of the Christ who will return. It assists you to experience *walking grace* throughout the season where lights burn
brightly, a grace that moves one along the path toward the reign

of God. This grace is like a constant Emmaus walk (see Luke 24:13–35). If you imagine walking gracefully through the season, it will encourage you to pay attention because God might just have a special grace on the road of your Emmaus journey, where hearts are quickened, not only in the breaking of the bread, but also in the symbols of the church celebrations.

The *Revised Common Lectionary* reminds people of the context of Christmas in this way: "The structure of the Christmas cycle presumes an Advent that is basically eschatological (looking forward to the return or second coming of the Lord Jesus and the realization of the reign of God) more than a season of preparation for Christmas (which recalls his first coming among us)."[20] As the prophesies of the Messiah the Jewish people expected are heard, they are listened to in the real expectation generated by the *not yet* of the second coming, which allows every person to approach the *already* of the first coming with fresh anticipation. The Messiah, Jesus the Christ for Christians, makes all things new.

Within the context of apocalyptic literature, you read of wars and famines, earthquakes and people fleeing. This may feel like a rude intrusion upon the music and dancing, the lights and mistletoe, the candles and branches. It will not be a disturbance if you remember that the final coming has three aspects:

1. The end of the cosmos as anticipated in all these destructions of evil
2. The crumbling of the religious system, symbolized by the Temple's destruction
3. The destruction of the individual's world in death[21]

Advent's message that God alone promises and sends the Messiah parallels the biblical apocalyptic message that the goodness of God is the only reliable source of security. That message is, indeed, cause for hope. It surpasses the security promised by high-paying jobs, big homes, healthy children, and three-car garages. That message rings true in the ears of those who have very little of this world's goods. It keeps them from despair.

Desmond Tutu in his work *Hope and Suffering* sermonizes about liberation from suffering, especially in reflection upon early slavery. The slaves believed that God was there from the beginning and God had dealings with the slaves' ancestors. God had made promises to the ancestors of the slaves. Some were fulfilled but some were not. The slaves might have thought that God had forgotten them or that God was not to be trusted. But, no, they continued to walk in the promise that God does not forget. The song by Carey Landry is an appropriate reminder of this theme: "I will never forget you my people. I have carved you on the palm of my hand....I will never forget my own."

Perhaps people cut short the memories of death, famine, and wars because they don't want to think of these realities. However, death is all around in the cycle of life so it can never be completely forgotten. It can be pushed out of memory for a while, but it has a strange way of moving into one's life very quickly. When it occurs, it can be managed with a foundation for endurance, the kind of staying power that upheld the victims of slavery.

In his work *Theology of Play*, Moltmann suggests that laughter is the medium between the inestimable magnitude of our tasks and the boundaries of our strength. Thus, hope is the virtue being sought at times of death, and laughter is the specific access into hope. Since laughter is more about being than doing, it urges people forward into complete trust of a God who is always present, a God who once journeyed with Moses and continues to journey with humanity until the reign of God comes.

The task of the Advent preacher or teacher is to assist in the integration of these concepts and eliminate the frightening responses that people often feel when hearing apocalyptic readings. Life is a continuous ebb and flow between birth and death. Facing both of these realities of the human condition with courage is the only way to live hopefully.

Paul reminds the people of God that they are saved by hope, even though hope cannot be seen. If people expect to see that future of hope, then what they see is not hope. Paul charges the faithful of God to hope for what they do not see, waiting in patience for that time of ultimate revelation (Rom 8:24–25). In the end, then, the preacher or teacher of the Advent cycle reminds people to live in hope and offers them the opportunity of practicing this perspective in daily life.[22]

In order to assist readers of this book to develop themselves into people of hope and courage, the next chapter highlights the plan for my life as teacher and preacher. The chapter includes two sermon samples of apocalyptic preaching, which emphasize courage and hope during times of crisis.

Apocalyptic literature is the story of
divine intervention
to set the wrongs right and
to correct the excessive optimism of the prophets.
The [reign of God] could come
only when God intervened
to create a new world on the ruins of the old.
— *Demetrius Dumm*[1]

Chapter Twelve

A PLAN FOR MY LIFE: PREACHING AND TEACHING

The excitement was electrifying! It was the first day of the new exhibit, "Masks: Faces of Culture," at the St. Louis Art Museum. The exhibit had been six years in the making. Curators traveled the globe gathering and even bargaining for masks.

The theme of masks reappeared in the St. Louis University theater department play, *A Company of Wayward Saints*. Nine masked characters improvised the story of humanity through the ages. Arguments among the cast caused the company to fold before intermission! After the break, performers slowly and shamefully returned, and removing masks, unfolded humanity's journey with a different perspective: birth to death.

These events surfaced excitement about a very familiar image: a white-faced "masked" mime. This image had been percolating rather strongly within as I pondered my theology of preaching, and I couldn't seem to let go of it. The "masks" exhibit and the stage play not only fascinated me, but also urged the image forward.

How do these experiences converge with a person's theology of preaching? Jeff Daniel, commenting on the "Masks" exhibit,

154

offers a helpful clue: "Mask is an equal opportunity accessory, a modifying device fit not only for the good, but for the bad and the ugly as well."[2] People in all cultures and societies have created masks for many reasons. The mask is a universal mode of transformation, for both practical and spiritual reasons. The mask's power allows the same white-faced character to play Satan as well as the Divine Spirit, the Pharisee as well as Jesus.

An artist dons a mask to tell a story and unmasks theological meanings. A teacher or preacher, artists with words, assists those who are learning to unmask both good and evil in order to choose wisely. The masked artist and the preacher/teacher do the same thing, "awakening and making explicit what is already there in the depths of [the person], not by nature but by grace."[3] For some courageous people, this awakening process, this unmasking, happens quickly, while for others, it happens much more slowly. Some people need more time to recognize grace. As a work of art, preachers and teachers must be careful not to do violence to people on their journey toward the God of mystery.

The theology of inclusiveness unmasked in the next chapter provides language that expands, not limits, imagination about who is to participate, especially in the preaching ministry. A new form of language, one that can imagine nonordained participation, is critical.

At the current time, in the Roman Catholic Church, opportunities for women are severely limited. However, I continue to embrace hope that eventually an authorization for such engagement will unfold. The preaching plan presented here gives identity to the formation of both preachers and teachers. By daring to plan, the unmasking continues, contemplating its fulfillment at a future time.

UNMASKING A VISION
THAT DEFINES A CALL

Masks are confining! They limit one's vision. One cannot envision unless one sees completely, because "what people see is an indication of what they care about and can care about."[4] I intensely wish to care, and therefore strive to see! Preachers and teachers must involve themselves in the process of unmasking, attempting to unmask those actions that will assist identification as compassionate, loving and feeling people, using all of themselves to live with an inclusive vision.

A vision is essentially spiritual, assisting us with a life of integrity. Teachers and preachers must envision a world in which a new humanity is always within reach, one in which people are defined by freedom, not oppression. How will such a world emerge? A simple yet complex answer is that people must be willing to seek truth by destroying existing relations of untruth.

One untruth is the impossibility of a truly inclusive community. The mysterious biblical journey of any preacher's or teacher's life indicates that the nature of *journey* is to liberate. This is confirmed by Eslinger, who says, "Distinctiveness of the biblical narrative…is in the character of the world it discloses—a world in which outcasts are sought and restored to community, sinners are forgiven, healing is found, and hospitality is extended and received."[5] Unmasking must happen in response to the story of freedom and hope within the biblical drama in spite of the oppression contained within its pages. This narrative also demands decisions about truth and discipleship. Following the radical Jesus will often make teachers and preachers of apocalyptic literature *excluded outsiders* as they choose to center their lives on the biblical text.

A short and extremely stark biblical text for this inspiring journey is the Gospel of Mark, a Gospel that has created an appetite for unmasking truth as praxis. It is complex in its portrayal of characters who choose to follow Jesus and those who refuse that invitation. In spite of that portrayal, a challenging message about being Christian is unmasked within its pages. One who dares to intensely read Mark's Gospel is taken on a profound journey, a "transforming journey of mind, moving from fear to protest to a word of Christ to a declaration of faith."[6]

The transforming journey is always *in process* as it engages more people in a preaching ministry, encompassing all segments of the church community in all aspects of preaching, including the eucharistic liturgy. *That* it happens is more important than *how* it happens! God calls preachers, so churches must find ways to educate those called, to test that call within the Christian community, and, ultimately, to affirm that call within a public context. The preacher who takes the call seriously, prayerfully encountering the biblical text and struggling with the implications of its message, assures the community that the truth comes from the Spirit. The dream will be fulfilled in a community of faith that hopes for the reign of God. Wasn't that also the vision of Jesus? John's Gospel expresses the inclusive community well, for it remembers the call of Jesus that all may be one in God (John 17:20–21).

How preachers can be sure of a call is a very engaging question for our day, especially since women have not been encouraged nor allowed, in most cases, to test that call within the Roman Catholic Church. Nevertheless, I must follow the call of the Spirit.

UNMASKING THE VISION THAT FORMS A SCRIPTURE INSTRUCTOR INTO A PREACHER

The Spirit-call to be named *Dorothy, preacher*, was awakened about five years ago by my brother Dominican, Jude Siciliano, OP. Afterward, nourished with a scripture-teaching ministry, opportunities to test that call began to emerge. The Dominican charism of study provided the path upon which to walk. Teaching scripture had been a form of preaching, but now there was something more God wanted from my formation.

Human experience has given shape to this call to preach, helping a dream come to fruition in strange ways. The call came in the midst of recovering a life story. What was once a masked life became unmasked, as the truth of a journey toward God was revealed within the scripture story: "When we place our story on top of the biblical story, we learn more about both."[7] Even though the journey is a lifelong search, the basic theology of scripture has been absorbed within my bones.

Education is now revealing further dimensions of that call, guiding thought, praxis, and methodology. A patient dialogue with experience, tradition, and culture assists in understanding how they integrate within the preaching moment. The absurdity of suffering leading to glory continues to shape this desire to preach. This paradox makes it tempting to don the mask over and over again. Because I am aware that this calling may entail a new type of suffering than previously experienced, courage will prevail with the help of God's grace. Since I am called to preach, I may be called to unique forms of suffering as I critically and prayerfully interpret the text in light of the tradition and confront the culture with the truth of that text.

Transformation is continual for me as I bear witness to God present within other people's struggles as well as my own. The biblical message cannot be spiritualized. The cross of Jesus is more real in the lives of the "have nots," who must fight each day for some dignity from the "haves" of society. It is so easy to spiritualize the cross, if I am not experiencing it daily. I realize that my call involves standing before the cross with truthfulness and embodying the gospel vision of inclusiveness.

UNMASKING A MISSION FOR PREACHING

Recently, dialogue with "hub symbols"[8] synthesized my core values. Only by faith have I been able to integrate a life story and apply it to an inclusive vision that each person must be treated with dignity. God created and all was good (Gen 1:1–31). God will continue to create through my good actions! This clarity of values has kept me from donning a mask and hiding. It is essential to be fully unmasked to both develop—and live—any mission. Unmasking has allowed the following mission statement for preaching and teaching to emerge:

This Roman Catholic Christian woman stands before a mysterious "Presence-in-Absence"[9] and lives the mission given in baptism by Jesus the Christ to be a hope-filled prophetic force in helping form an inclusive community of faith. Commitment as a Dominican Sister, following the call of Dominic *to contemplate and to give to others the fruits of that contemplation* directs the mission. A new Word from God is shared, moving it away from domination and control and toward equality in order to transform the world. Authority has been given to unmask the powers[10] of injustice by reason of a baptismal sharing in the passion, death, and resurrection of Jesus the Christ. This authority remains authentic within a daily unmasking of the need for conversion, while allowing the Spirit of God to transform a fragile heart. It is possible for words to become inauthentic if approached in a nonchalant way that forgets to *tremble* in the presence of the Mystery. This authentic preacher of God's Word is willing to walk on the prophetic edge, with or without a safety net, and be exposed to the process of victimization, both in the preaching event and in the action that follows from preaching.

OPPORTUNITIES MASKED WITH THREATS, STRENGTHS UNMASKED BY WEAKNESSES

Since I tend toward pessimism when it comes to our current church and world situation, opportunities often seem limited. At those times, I remember that Jesus worked on a small scale but did great things. He knew the power of images and embedded them in parables, working on the principle that changing minds will bring the *Kin-dom*.

Flashbacks of this same image power occur within, assisting me to remember scripture teaching experiences, where every day brought people of hope, openness of heart, and a willingness to be formed in faith, even though they struggled with tough issues that faced them in life. They hungered to know the word of God and to allow it to make an impact on them. These virtuous people faithfully heard the story of their lives with a stance of hospitality, freedom, forgiveness, and a huge capacity of heart that helped them see many possibilities for their future. Healthy and wholesome vulnerability existed within these students. In essence, these people of God shaped opportunities for success within me, a preacher *in process*.

On the other hand, I cannot be naïve. Conflict is to be expected and could block the path to the Kin-dom. The warning I received came from a preacher/teacher who indicated that "people who experience no conflict do not think theologically; they simply repeat what others have said."[11]

I know that I could be a willing hostage to my past and, thus, limit myself as I face a changing future that moves our world closer to the reign of God. I know that the current time needs creative and imaginative people. This is my preaching gift, and I hope it will stir within the church so that stagnation will not move God to speak again that a revelation of the Lord may be uncommon and visions often infrequent (1 Sam 3:1b).

A preaching/teaching mission will be somewhat ineffective if constantly faced with those who find it impossible to accept the gift of a common humanity and who dismiss community rather than seek it. Those who discard the fact that freedom must be for everybody or it will be for nobody may attempt to negate the prophetic task of any preacher or teacher, interpreting the truth of the gospel for our times.

The searching journey of this preacher-in-process has shown that weaknesses transformed into strengths counteract such opposition! In the second letter to the Corinthian Christians, Paul teaches, "My grace is sufficient for you, for power is made perfect in weakness" (2 Cor 12:9a). Yes, I am able to name important strengths, but I am amazed that these most often come from remembering perceived weaknesses. I know that extreme vulnerability learned from suffering will assist me in evaluating structures that lead to injustices.

Strength also comes from membership in the Grand Rapids Dominican Sisters, where a global network is created, since all sisters carry the achievements of any one sister. This network strives to unmask systems of oppression and dreams of a better future for all. It provides impetus for this prophetic ministry on the edge.

Two sermons are presented following. I preached the first sermon on a Sunday before the Advent season began. A master preacher presented the other shortly after the 9/11, often-thought-of apocalyptic, crisis. Both are given here as sermons that exemplify the themes of this book.

SAMPLE PREACHING FROM TWO APOCALYPTIC TEXTS

33rd Sunday in Ordinary Time[12]

Watercolor painting is extremely impressionistic. Artists create images from symbols, choosing "right" colors to speak a message with their painting. In a similar way, words often give us brush-strokes of color.

Listen to these newspaper stories near the end of the century. What colors were created by them?

August 8, 1999

Four-year-old Ismail Cimen is pulled from the rubble of the Turkish earthquake after six days. His relatives had given up hope and were preparing a grave. But Ismail never gave up hope. He was dubbed a "miracle of God" because of his will to live, defying the "limits" of human survival.

August 25, 1999

Yaguine and Fode, African teenagers, are found frozen to death in the bay of the landing gear of a Sabina airliner. The boys knew the risk, but a note in their belongings suggested that they never gave up hope. "We suffer enormously in Africa. Help us! We lack rights as children. We have war and illness. We lack food. We lack education. We want to study. Help us study in Africa so we can be like you." These young men reached in death an audience that eluded them in life.

September 26, 1999

Thirteen-year-old Hero Joy Nightingale, who can neither speak nor walk, designed an Internet magazine that boasted readers in seventy-seven countries. Unable to perform complex muscle movements, Hero's arms were supported so she could communicate. Her first edition spoke hope for the disabled:

"People are [often] unable to see past my disability, see the whole of me. [But] I am alive, well and kicking."

These headlines before the year 2000 were colored with hope in the midst of tragedy. These children painted watercolor displays with their dreams…and their actions. On the one hand, they knew that hope colored their lives. On the other hand, they knew that the hope that sustained their dreams did not negate the colors of disorientation and terror.

Now, we stand on the brink of 2001. We soon begin another Advent. What headlines will color our hope and sustain us for the days of turmoil that we might face?

Today's biblical readings are brushstrokes of hope that help energize communities mired in terror. Yes, they do paint fears of concerned people: Many will come in my name and will deceive you.…There will be wars, earthquakes, famine.…These begin the birth-pangs. But they also give hope of God's promise.…God's people will be spared.…Christ has taken his seat at God's right hand.…Our birthright is in God.

The people of the readings were like the children of the headlines. Their lives were a watercolor of dreams and their actions painted hope in the midst of great anxiety. The writer of Daniel saw the reign of Antiochus IV destroying people's dreams. So Daniel paints hope that the reign of terror would soon end. The writer of Mark's Gospel feared the destruction of Jerusalem. But Mark also pictures God saving the faithful ones.

What colors will you and I, people of the new millennium, paint for future generations? Will the pain of the world overwhelm us? Or will we keep steady in the hope we profess? Will we lack dreams for a better future? Or will we trust that God promises to save us?

Make *no* mistake! The attitudes we take from these readings will color our future. What color will it be for you—and me? A brushstroke of fear…or a brushstroke of hope?

Sample Homily in an Apocalyptic-like Time[13]

In light of today's awesome text from the Gospel of Luke (6:27–38), I have chosen to say a few things about democracy and a Christian understanding of nonviolence.

On the subject of democracy, Methodist theologian Walter Wink says this: "Ideally, democracy is nonviolence institutionalized. It is the only political system that rejects domination in principle and grounds itself in equality before the law."

From what little I know about terrorist theory, even though an event such as we have experienced this week is planned over a long period of time, it is executed on very short notice, perhaps weeks or perhaps many months after remote preparation is complete. We may never know why this Tuesday was chosen to execute these terrorist acts, but at a level of meaning I can't help but think it significant that just last week, the United States chose to walk out of the international conference on racism in Durban, South Africa. At some level, last week the United States refused to listen to what the world was trying to say to us about our stance toward the Palestinian people.

Whoever is responsible for this week's terrorist acts in New York and Washington is certainly a master of myth. In these two very phallic acts, an affront was made both to the center of international and American capitalism and to the American military. Anybody who is listening knows this to be true. But can we also listen to these acts at a level at which the perpetrators could not have intended, seeing in these acts also an affront to democracy and to a nonviolent rule of law?[14]

Our text today says, "Do unto others as you would have them do unto you." This sentence and today's text may be the most fundamental statement of nonviolence in the whole Bible. However, as we listen to the words of the Golden Rule, it would behoove us to consider the dark underside of this sentence. When this sentence is involuted or turned inside out through violence, it can read, "Become what you hate." I was shaken this morning to read in huge type on the front page of the *St. Louis Post Dispatch* the word *avenge*. Terrible violence has been done to us, and we now have serious choices to make, lest by revenge we become what we hate.

In three pithy sentences, today's text calls us to attend to the weightier matters of the Law: justice, mercy, and love. I always remember the words of the Golden Rule as my father said them: "Do as you would be done by." We would do well in the year ahead to take seriously a study of the several criteria of the Just

War theory. First, there must be a *just cause*, and this week on that score we certainly can agree. With regard to *legitimate authority* and *formal declaration*, the Congress of the United States is in session on this question at this very moment.

The harder consideration, however, has to do with the remaining four criteria: a just war must be conducted with *peaceful intention*, as a *last resort*, with *reasonable hope of success*, and with *means proportionate to the ends*. As we hear these criteria and as we pray for the president, the National Security Council, the members of Congress, and our military leaders, we beg God to give them the wisdom of Solomon.

In another pithy sentence, which touches on the subject of mercy, our passage says, "Do not judge." As I hear this admonition of Jesus, I am proud to be a Dominican. Not that others, of course, do not also have this experience, but as we Dominicans think about this crisis, we are well aware of our Dominican sisters and brothers in Pakistan, in Afghanistan, and in Iraq. These Dominicans are not fleeing those countries. Rather, they remain to minister to their people, and in doing so they remind us that at the most fundamental level of our humanity, we all are one. We all are one.

And in the weighty matter of love, our passage says, "Love your enemies." Martin Luther King Jr. preached on this passage at least once each year. Each year he reflected on the command to love our enemies. And of course Martin Luther King chose to lay down his life. He preached knowingly on this subject of his own death, just days before he died. In this aspect, Martin Luther King was exactly like the terrorists on those airplanes, who also laid down their lives.

However, we know that Martin Luther King was an assiduous student of Mahatma Gandhi, who in turn was a student of the nonviolence of Jesus. I am always startled to be reminded at how often Gandhi said, "It is always better to be violent than to be cowardly." But Gandhi always went on to say that he would never resort to violence. Gandhi taught us that religious nonviolence is never passive. It is courageous and intelligent, and it often involves the practice of nonlethal coercion. No less than the in-your-face acts of violence we have witnessed in New York and

Washington, religious nonviolence is also in-your-face action, but for the sake of a just rule of law.

When confronted with this week's violence, I certainly understand the impulse to respond violently. In my mind and in my gut I know the compelling impulse that says violent response to violence is necessary. Yet, as a Christian scholar, I also know this impulse to be a myth and untrue. The gospel demands justice, nonviolently and through the rule of law. In the last century some 110 million people died violently, more than had died cumulatively by violence in the previous five thousand years combined. How I wish the nations of the Earth could work together through nonviolent coercive action to turn terrorists over to court, without becoming what we hate, without escalating the cycle of violence. We are in a worldwide race against the terrible effects of the escalating cycle of violence. We must find another way. When will the violence stop? When will the violence stop?

By way of conclusion, I would like to read an eloquent and brief entry from today's Dominican News Service on the World Wide Web:

> On September 11, the United States of America was subjected to an incredibly horrible terrorist attack. As preachers of the Good News of Jesus Christ, let us join together in this moment more strongly to pray to God for the victims of hatred and to work more diligently to overcome hatred in the world.
>
> Those who hate are like lost sheep who have wandered far away from the God of Love. But Jesus, the Good Shepherd, went after the lost sheep. As we care for the victims of those who hate, let us also reach out to those who are victims of their own hatred. In Christ's name, let us seek not only to end the suffering caused by hatred, but to end hatred itself, comforting the widows and newly made orphans, but also let us seek out the lost sheep. People are not the enemy. Hatred itself is the real Enemy.

Since the concept of hope threaded its way through the entire book, the last chapter concludes that perspective with some reflections on my theology of preaching. Chapter 13 shows how I retain hope during the seemingly hopeless time in which we are now entrenched.

165

What, then, are we to say about these things?
If God is for us, who is against us?
The one who did not withhold the only Son,
but gave him up for all of us,
will that one not give us everything?
— *Romans 8:31–33 (adapted)*

Chapter Thirteen

THEOLOGY OF PREACHING/TEACHING[1]

On December 22, 2003, I happened to turn on *The Oprah Winfrey Show*. I have watched this show before and know of its power to touch lives. That show touched my hopeful heart and I would like it to touch yours as well.

The Oprah show that day was entitled "Christmas Kindness." It was about Oprah's trip to South Africa for Christmas 2002. Oprah told us about that venture because, as she says, it profoundly touched her heart and she wanted the show to express how it might touch our hearts as well. She said that, if we were able to reach out, it would bring immeasurable joy to our lives as it has to hers.[2]

"It was so overwhelming that I wish I could take them all with me," stated Oprah.[3] Thousands of children's lives were touched by this trip to South Africa. Many of those children have been orphaned because of the rampant spread of AIDS in the land. Oprah knew that she gave many children hope by bringing food, clothing, toys, and school supplies to them. Nevertheless, Oprah realized that what she gave was miniscule compared to what the children gave to her. "It is irreplaceable," Oprah promised us.[4] If we reach out to children and give them a little hope, the world will be a different place.

This chapter promises to build your hope so that you are able to reach out in some way. It is dedicated to Oprah and to her children from South Africa. It is also dedicated to all those who will reach out because they have been inspired in countless other ways.

UNMASKING FOR RELATING TO GOD

Moses understood that masking was the normal way of encountering God. Moses heard a mysterious voice and saw miraculous signs from this Divine Being, but he only saw God's back in the meeting tent (Exod 3:14, 33:23). Humans might try to stand unmasked, attempting to know God by using human concepts, human words, and human images. These efforts slightly unveil the divine, for human experience speaks only analogously to divine reality. The transcendent being sought is holy mystery. Thus, we can never "wrap [our] mind completely around this mystery and exhaust divine reality in words and concepts."[5]

Humans take off masks courageously when their search for God becomes an ongoing journey *toward* God. For the spiritual seeker, God emerges in the "relationship between our questioning selves and the unexplainability of things."[6] Those who have followed a spiritual path know how difficult it is to take off a mask and allow for complete openness to God's Spirit. Persons lull themselves into thinking they know God but then are surprised when God becomes a source of further questioning. The journey involves continual wonder and also frightening dependency. In the end, the initiative is God's. We are God's partners in faith.

The great accomplishment of this process is that faith can be developed in an unmasked state. With eyes wide open, persons embark on a search for truth. The journey begins with the experience of beauty. There is beauty in creation. Spend a day at the botanical garden and find God. There is beauty in relationships. Break bread with a friend and find God. If a friend is not available, meet a stranger and find God. Open yourself to beauty found in scripture, find your journey to be like the journey described in its pages, and there you will also see the face of God. These images are the essence of the Emmaus journey (Luke 24:13–35).

We must be unmasked to participate in such a journey. The search for God is never abstract. Persons are not just observers, unless they refuse to take off their masks for an exciting journey. If persons are afraid of this dimension of the journey, perhaps they need a more concrete image of God, the one found in Jesus Christ. What difference would the image of Jesus make to our masked seeker?

UNMASKING FOR RELATING TO JESUS THE CHRIST

Is it possible to take off our masks to encounter the immanent God revealed in Jesus Christ? From early on, theology developed an understanding of Jesus by imagining a God moving in complete openness toward the fulfillment of creation. That openness outpoured onto creation with a person, Jesus, who was also identified with Sophia, the spirit of wisdom. This description was used, not only for the risen and exalted Christ, but also for the historical Jesus.

The humanity of Jesus became exalted in the image of Sophia. That exaltation is manifested through followers of Jesus today. Unmasking allows us to love God by loving a particular person, Jesus of Nazareth, and emulating that person in our own life. It takes considerable inner strength to be unmasked for this journey, as our focus will necessarily become solidarity with the whole suffering human race, emphasizing the intent of the christological doctrine to continue being inclusive. However, the unmasking will be well worth the effort.

This unmasked journey enables us to walk authentically with the *wrong persons* and in the *wrong places*. In the Gospels, Jesus is constantly shown eating with sinners, healing lepers and others who were on the margins of society as well as calling disciples who were not of the power elite. Jesus was, indeed, a political revolutionary because he constantly transgressed boundaries. His actions always had political implications.

The theology of the cross that emerged in early Christianity is intimately tied to this tension and embraces the most marginal in society. The cross is truly inclusive. It discloses the dignity of all persons, especially those on the margins, because it proclaims the victory of life over death. Roberto Goizueta, focusing upon Hispanic Americans, poignantly describes how they embrace the cross as an "eerie scene...not an event that happened two thousand years ago, but an event taking place and [one] in which [the people] are actively participating."[7] The Hispanic people approach the cross fully unmasked, for they know that the cross describes the reality of their lives. The cross shows a God who is acting dramatically in those who are weak and dying, in those who have exhausted their resources and are allowing God to fully lead them, in those who are most vulnerable and have surrendered to divine love. For these suffering people, belief in the resurrection of Jesus is belief in God's justice, a justice that vindicates and affirms the life and example of Jesus. Thus, Jesus embodies God's desire for people to live rightly. This desire is inclusive. Sacramental anthropology must be inclusive as well.

UNMASKING FOR RELATING IN COMMUNITY: INCLUSIVENESS OF HUMAN LIBERATION

Living inclusive sacramental community is difficult, certainly within the United States today, where the strongest impulse is toward individualism. Persons are often tempted to wear masks to survive. However, masking prevents us from noticing the interconnectedness and interdependence of all humanity. Individualism so often veils the fact that humans are dependent upon social, political, and economic realities for survival. Therefore, people who live with masks tend to build fences instead of bridges, blocking themselves from true human encounter and encounter with God too!

Masks are rarely simple, for they may have multiple meanings. Recently, a newspaper article told of a judge's decision to allow the Ku Klux Klan to demonstrate in New York City only if they removed their masks. It was feared that wearing masks would lead to violent demonstration. So—masks may be adopted for violence. This brings to mind a serious question: How are masks used in human community?

Jesus' words and actions call Christians to inclusive community. Within faith communities, believers are exhorted to unmask their lives and become vulnerable to others. Within faith communities, the art of receiving and giving love are both required. These are difficult tasks, indeed, but absolutely necessary for the full flowering of humanity. Christian conversion is essential to growth, for it unmasks those who turn toward God and away from sin. An open person becomes more inclusive while turning toward God, for, in the process, one turns toward the human community, toward creation, and toward one's deepest truth. Inclusiveness drives away violence as we turn from sin, for, while turning, we also move away from those still encased in their masks, living as people of the lie. Christian conversion is ongoing, as tensions between trust and untrustworthiness as well as sin and grace constantly challenge us to "let go and let God." Such conversion unmasks signs of God's grace, found everywhere in our world. We must look with eyes wide open to discover these signs. Perhaps that won't even be enough. Jesus talks about people who look and look but never notice. Thus he teaches in parables (Mark 4:10–12).

It is essential that people be free and unique individuals in order to assist in building community. Roberto Goizueta uses the term "theology of accompaniment" to describe the use of our individuality for the betterment of community. He states that Hispanic people, often coming from exile and abandonment, have nurtured the conviction that people do not, and cannot, live in isolation from each other.

Thus, it is only within healthy, unmasked communities that believers are able to find interpretive clues to what is happening in their lives and in the world around them. As individuals discover an inner sense of authority, they are able to build self-confidence and self-esteem, which leads to liberation from an unhealthy, masked self. Thus, the path to an inclusive sacramental community is a real dying, a powerful unmasking of self. If we are able to participate in such growth, it will lead to a resurrection and a new Pentecost within the Christian community. E. E. Cummings summarizes this profound journey as follows: "We can never be born enough, we are human beings; for whom birth is a supremely welcome mystery, the mystery of growing: the mystery which happens only and whenever we are faithful to ourselves."[8]

UNMASKING FOR LIVING RIGHT RELATIONSHIPS

The theology of human community just described is ideal—something for which we never stop striving. It is often hindered by the human condition of selfishness. Human systems have been created and sustained that promote the oppression of vast numbers of people. The need to dominate or enslave others is deeply embedded in social systems. A way must be found to live in a community that is candid in unmasking a crippling domination system that includes racism, sexism, ageism, classism, homophobia, and a lack of awareness of our ecological and cosmic problems. Critical theologians today must ask new questions to unmask complex issues facing our world at the dawn of a new millennium. The path into a new future demands moving away from whatever encourages aggressive and competitive behaviors toward that which nurtures cooperative behaviors.

Liberation theologian Roberto Goizueta was convincing in his suggestion of exposing people to many cultures. Especially in the United States, people must unmask the anxiety created by the need to control others, apparent in a number of current attitudes, such as the attitude toward immigrants. Openness to other cultures is impossible when one culture holds all the keys to economic and political power. The dominant culture will too often impose its values and way of life on other peoples, blocking the development of *mestizaje*, a Spanish term used to describe the ability to be culturally mixed. The dominant culture in the United States is so powerfully entrenched that any differences are threatening. Racial and cultural purity is often carried to an extreme: we cannot be *both* black and white; we must be *either* black or white. Unmasking this inability to be both culturally and racially diverse is one contribution liberation theology makes to the work of the church. Preachers and teachers are called to authenticity in their commitment to social justice. This is a precondition for Christian ministry. Teachers and preachers must assist in eradicating boundaries that inhibit God's reign from continuing development within our world.

Feminist theologian Elizabeth Johnson offers compelling arguments that it is critical for people to be exposed to the concept of feminine mutuality. Christians are called to read society from the perspective of its victims, counteracting aggression and competition. Besides people of other cultures and races, women are too often victims of the dominant culture. It is clear as history is read that women were "taught to think as men, to identify with a male point of view, and to accept as normal and legitimate a male system of values,"[9] masking their true identities. Changes did occur in the twentieth century, but obscuring women's gifts continues. This historical discounting must end if we are to ever construct an inclusive society.

It has not been salvific to diminish the image of God in women by designating them as symbols of temptation and evil. It has not been salvific to use the cross as a poignant symbol of patriarchy. Feminist theology advocates the reform of the patriarchal, civil, and ecclesial structures that support sexism in order that just relationships will lead to a more inclusive sacramental community. Feminist theology needs the critical thinking of both women *and* men.

Unmasking the logic that supports an all-male language system is essential and can only be done through a careful analysis of language. Some people argue that "God is not male" while, at the same time, refusing to use feminine imagery for God and refusing to use inclusive language for humanity. They have grown comfortable with masks that have blinded them to the power of language in forming values and attitudes. Others, unaware that they are speaking in male terminology, must be assisted in becoming more conscientious language users. Johnson suggests only one valid solution: to seek speech about God in which fullness of both female and male humanity as well as cosmic reality may serve as divine symbol in equivalent ways.

An inclusive sacramental anthropology asks, How can the exercise of human power and authority be more like the exercise of divine power and authority? Limitations imposed by the dominant hierarchical system have masked those who want to live with hope by diminishing their imaginations. Wisdom comes from dialogue among those willing to serve the needs of all humanity. Preachers and teachers have a critical role to play in this venture. If we are vulnerable as we listen to the voice of God through the scriptures, we will enable divine action to lead us and those we serve to embrace a more inclusive sacramental community.

FACING CRITICAL ISSUES AS UNMASKED AND HOPEFUL

Critical issues in today's society will need the efforts of those willing to live *"on the edge."* Unjust global situations are at an all-time high. Often these situations have resulted in violence. As we ended the past century, history has shown it to be the most violent century of all time.[10] A prophetic preaching and teaching ministry is needed to unmask the causes of violence by identifying the sociopolitical structures responsible for that violence. Black liberation theologian James Cone severely criticizes the churches for not taking more responsibility for change of society. A poem entitled "Listen Christians," used at a poor people's rally, exemplifies the noneffectiveness of the churches: "I was hungry...I was imprisoned...I was naked...and you prayed, discussed and formed committees."[11]

Scripture calls followers of Jesus to be concerned about those in need (Luke 4:18). We must be courageous in siding with the victims in order to transform civilization. A broken, yet risen, community of faith lives in hope as its ministers, fed by the word of God, preach and teach a new world in which value systems are turned upside down (see Luke 2:46–55 and 1 Sam 2:1–10).

It is critical to reach out to spiritually hungry young people who are wary of membership in institutional churches that have not proved trustworthy. Christian churches must unmask and ask *why* young people do not find them trustworthy. It is imperative that courageous unmasking occurs in order to find ways to reach out to hungry young people and feed their spiritual needs.

Evangelization efforts will demand from teachers and preachers an ability to listen carefully, to model conversion as well as invite to conversion, to connect as community, and to worship meaningfully. Studies show that young people, when respected, have zeal for living that can be harnessed for good. They will be attracted to the cross as the symbol of overcoming conflict as long as their mentor-preachers and teachers are willing to take off their own masks at the foot of the cross. By doing this, we show that strength comes from submitting to the one who gave his life in violence in order to overcome violence.

There is critical need to encourage young people to commit their lives to the prophetic task of unmasking the world's injustices. The church has suffered through years of decreased vocations, while young people have volunteered service in record numbers. Has the recent upswing in vocations shown that they find religious more worthy of respect? Only time will tell.

I have laid out a plan and a theology of inclusiveness that was called forth from the hope generated by a study of apocalyptic literature. Where do we go from here? How do we produce the critical thinking that unmasks the systemic change needed to resolve the world's crises? This work calls upon teachers and preachers to assist this task by being authentic witnesses of God's Word to those hungering for that in which they can believe. The time is short—and the task is great. We must each do our part. May the hopefulness of the apocalyptic writers thrust us forward into a new world of peace, cooperation, and love.

Appendix: Apocalyptic Texts on Sundays and Major Feasts

FOUR LECTIONARIES (YEAR A)[1]

Italicized biblical references are apocalyptic texts.

Revised Common	Roman Catholic	Episcopal
1st Sunday of Advent Isaiah 2:1–5 Romans 13:11–14 *Matthew 24:36–44*	**1st Sunday of Advent** Isaiah 2:1–5 Romans 13:11–14 *Matthew 24:37–44*	**1st Sunday of Advent** Isaiah 2:1–5 Romans 13:8–14 *Matthew 24:37–44*
The Transfiguration Exodus 24:12–18 2 Peter 1:16–21 Matthew 17:1–9	**The Transfiguration** *Daniel 7:9–10, 13–14* 2 Peter 1:16–19 Matthew 17:1–9	**The Transfiguration** Exodus 24:12 (13–14) 15–18 Philippians 3:7–14 Matthew 17:1–9
The Ascension Acts 1:1–11 Ephesians 1:15–23 Luke 24:44–53	**The Ascension** Acts 1:1–11 Ephesians 1:17–23 Matthew 28:19–20	**The Ascension** Acts 1:1–11, *Daniel 7:9–14* Ephesians 1:15–23 Acts 1:1–11 Luke 24:49–53 Mark 16:9–15, 19–20
7th Sunday of Easter Acts 1:6–14 1 Peter 4:12–14, 5:6–11 John 17:1–11	**7th Sunday of Easter** Acts 1:12–14 1 Peter 4:13–16 John 17:1–11	**7th Sunday of Easter** Acts 1:1–7 *Ezekiel 39:21–29* 1 Peter 4:12–19 Acts 1:1–7 (8–14) John 17:1–11
7th Sunday after Pentecost (Lutheran) (no apocalyptic in RCL) *Zechariah 9:9–12* Romans 7:15–25a Matthew 11:25–30	**14th Sunday in Ordinary Time** *Zechariah 9:9–10* Romans 8:9, 11–13 Matthew 11:25–30	**Proper 9** *Zechariah 9:9–12* Romans 7:21–8:6 Matthew 11:25–30

Revised Common	Roman Catholic	Episcopal
21st Sunday after Pentecost (Lutheran) (no apocalyptic in RCL) *Isaiah 25:6–10* Philippians 4:4–13 Matthew 22:1–10 (11–14)	**28th Sunday in Ordinary Time** *Isaiah 25:6–10* Philippians 4:12–14, 19–20 Matthew 22:1–14	**Proper 23** *Isaiah 25:1–9* Philippians 4:4–13 Matthew 22:1–14
Proper 24 Exodus 33:12–23 *1 Thessalonians 1:1–10* Matthew 22:15–22	**29th Sunday in Ordinary Time** Isaiah 45:1, 4–6 *1 Thessalonians 1:1–5* Matthew 22:15–21	**Proper 24** Isaiah 45:1–7 *1 Thessalonians 1:1–10* Matthew 22:15–22
22nd Sunday after Pentecost (Lutheran) Proper 25 Deuteronomy 34:1–12 *1 Thessalonians 2:1–8* Matthew 22:34–46	**30th Sunday in Ordinary Time** Exodus 22:20–26 *1 Thessalonians 1:5–10* Matthew 22:34–40	**Proper 25** Exodus 22:21–27 *1 Thessalonians 2:1–8* Matthew 22:34–46
23rd Sunday after Pentecost (Lutheran) Leviticus 19:1–2, 15–18 *1 Thessalonians 1:5b–10* Matthew 22:34–40 (41–46)		
Proper 26 Joshua 3:7–17 *1 Thessalonians 2:9–13* Matthew 23:1–12	**31st Sunday in Ordinary Time** Malachi 1:14–2:2, 8–10 *1 Thessalonians 2:7–9, 13* Matthew 23:1–12	**Proper 26** Micah 3:5–12 *1 Thessalonians 2:9–13, 17–20* Matthew 23:1–12
24th Sunday after Pentecost (Lutheran) Amos 5:18–24 *1 Thessalonians 4:13–14 (15–18) Matthew 25:1–13*		
Proper 27 Joshua 24:1–3a, 14–25 *1 Thessalonians 4:13–18 Matthew 25:1–13*	**32nd Sunday in Ordinary Time** Wisdom 6:12–16 *1 Thessalonians 4:13–18 Matthew 25:1–13*	**Proper 27** Amos 5:18–24 *1 Thessalonians 4:13–18 Matthew 25:1–13*

Revised Common	Roman Catholic	Episcopal
25th Sunday after Pentecost (Lutheran) Hosea 11:1–4, 8–9 *1 Thessalonians 5:1–11* *Matthew 25:14–30*		
Proper 28 Judges 4:1–7 *1 Thessalonians 5:1 11* *Matthew 25:14–30*	**33rd Sunday in Ordinary Time** Proverbs 31:10–13, 19–20, 30 31 *1 Thessalonians 5:1–6* *Matthew 25:14–30*	**Proper 28** Zephaniah 1:7, 12–18 *1 Thessalonians 5:1–10* *Matthew 25:14–15, 19–29*
26th Sunday after Pentecost (Lutheran) Malachi 2:1–2, 4–10 *1 Thessalonians 2:8–13* Matthew 23:1–12		
27th Sunday after Pentecost (Lutheran) Jeremiah 26:1–6 Matthew 24:1–14 *1 Thessalonians 3:7–13*		
All Saints' Sunday *Revelation 7:9–17* 1 John 3:1–3 Matthew 5:1–12	**All Saints' Sunday** *Revelation 7:2–4, 9–14* 1 John 3:1–3 Matthew 5:1–12	**All Saints' Sunday** Sirach 44:1–10, 13–14 *Revelation 7:2–4, 9–17* Matthew 5:1–12
(Lutheran) *Isaiah 26:1–4, 8–9* *12–13, 19–21* *Revelation 21:9–11* *22–27 (22:1–5)* Matthew 5:1–12		
Christ the King Proper 29 Ezekiel 34:11–16, 20–24 Ephesians 1:15–23 *Matthew 25:31–46*	**Christ the King 34th Sunday in Ordinary Time** Ezekiel 34:11–12, 15–17 1 Corinthians 15:20–26, 28 *Matthew 25:31–46*	**Christ the King Proper 29** Ezekiel 34:11–17 1 Corinthians 15:20–28 *Matthew 25:31–46*
(Lutheran) Ezekiel 34:11–16, 23–24 1 Corinthians 15:20–28 *Matthew 25:31–46*		

THREE LECTIONARIES (YEAR B)

Revised Common	Roman Catholic	Episcopal
1st Sunday of Advent Isaiah 64:1–9 1 Corinthians 1:3–9 *Mark 13:24–37*	**1st Sunday of Advent** Isaiah 63:16b–17, 64:1, 3b–8 1 Corinthians 1:3–9 *Mark 13:33–37*	**1st Sunday of Advent** Isaiah 64:1–9a 1 Corinthians 1:1–9 *Mark 13:(24–32) 33–37*
3rd Sunday of Advent Isaiah 61:1–4, 8–11 *1 Thessalonians 5:16–24* John 1:6–8, 19–28	**3rd Sunday of Advent** Isaiah 61:1–2, 10–11 *1 Thessalonians 5:16–24* John 1:6–8, 19–28	**3rd Sunday of Advent** Isaiah 65:17–25 *1 Thessalonians 5:(12–15)* *16–28* John 1:6–8, 19–28 or John 3:23–30
The Transfiguration 2 Kings 2:1–12 2 Corinthians 4:3–6 Mark 9:2–9	**The Transfiguration** *Daniel 7:9–10, 13–14* 2 Peter 1:16–19 Mark 9:2–9	**The Transfiguration** 1 Kings 19:9–18 2 Peter 1:16–19 (20–21) Mark 9:2–9
Proper 9 *2 Samuel 5:1–5, 9–10* 2 Corinthians 12:2–10 Mark 6:1–13	**14th Sunday in Ordinary Time** *Ezekiel 2:2–5* 2 Corinthians 12:7–10 Mark 6:1–6	**Proper 9** *Ezekiel 2:1–7* 2 Corinthians 12:2–10 Mark 6:1–6
Proper 28 1 Samuel 1:4–20 Hebrews 10:11–14 (15–18) 19–25 *Mark 13:1–8*	**33rd Sunday in Ordinary Time** *Daniel 12:1–3* Hebrews 10:11–14, 18 *Mark 13:24–32*	**Proper 28** *Daniel 12:1–4a (5–13)* Hebrews 10:31–39 *Mark 13:14–23*
All Saints' Sunday Isaiah 25:6–9 *Revelation 21:1–6a* John 11:32–44	**All Saints' Sunday** *Revelation 7:2–4, 9–12* 1 John 3:1–3 Matthew 5:1–12	**All Saints' Sunday** Sirach 44:1–10, 13–14 *Revelation 7:2–4, 9–17* Matthew 5:1–12
Christ the King Proper 29 2 Samuel 23:1–7 *Revelation 1:4b–8* John 18:33–37	**Christ the King 34th Sunday in Ordinary Time** *Daniel 7:13–14* *Revelation 1:5–8* John 18:33–37	**Christ the King Proper 29** *Daniel 7:9–14* *Revelation 1:1–8* John 18:33–37

THREE LECTIONARIES (YEAR C)

Revised Common	Roman Catholic	Episcopal
1st Sunday of Advent Jeremiah 33:14–16 *1 Thessalonians 3:9–13* *Luke 21:25–36*	**1st Sunday of Advent** Jeremiah 33:14–16 *1 Thessalonians 3:12–4:2* *Luke 21:25–28, 34–36*	**1st Sunday of Advent** *Zechariah 14:4–9* *1 Thessalonians 3:9–13* *Luke 21:25–31*
The Transfiguration Exodus 34:29–35 2 Corinthians 3:12–4:2 Luke 9:28–36 (37–43)	**The Transfiguration** *Daniel 7:9–10* 2 Peter 1:16–19 Luke 9:28–36	**The Transfiguration** Exodus 34:29–35 1 Corinthians 12:27–13:13 Luke 9:28–36
2nd Sunday of Easter Acts 5:27–32 *Revelation 1:4–8* John 20:19–31	**2nd Sunday of Easter** Acts 5:12–16 *Revelation 1:9–13, 17–19* John 20:19–31	**2nd Sunday of Easter** Acts 5:12a, 17–22, 25–29 *Revelation 1:(1–8) 9–19* John 20:19–31
3rd Sunday of Easter Acts 9:1–6 (7–20) *Revelation 5:11–14* John 21:1–19	**3rd Sunday of Easter** Acts 5:27–32, 40–41 *Revelation 5:11–14* John 21:1–19	**3rd Sunday of Easter** Acts 9:1–19a *Revelation 5:6–14* John 21:1–14
4th Sunday of Easter Acts 9:36–43 *Revelation 7:9–17* John 10:22–30	**4th Sunday of Easter** Acts 13:14, 43–52 *Revelation 7:9, 14–17* John 10:27–30	**4th Sunday of Easter** Acts 13:15–16, 26–33 (34–39) *Revelation 7:9–17* John 10:22–30
5th Sunday of Easter Acts 11:1–18 *Revelation 21:1–6* John 13:31–35	**5th Sunday of Easter** Acts 14:21–27 *Revelation 21:1–5* John 13:31–35	**5th Sunday of Easter** Acts 13:44–52 *Revelation 19:1, 4–9* John 13:31–35
6th Sunday of Easter Acts 16:9–15 *Revelation 21:10, 22–22:5* John 14:23–29	**6th Sunday of Easter** Acts 15:1–2, 22–29 *Revelation 21:10–14, 22–23* John 14:23–29	**6th Sunday of Easter** Acts 14:8–18 *Revelation 21:22–22:5* John 14:23–29
7th Sunday of Easter Acts 16:16–34 *Revelation 22:12–14,* *16–17, 20–21* John 17:20–26	**7th Sunday of Easter** Acts 7:55–60 *Revelation 22:12–14,* *16–17, 20* John 17:20–26	**7th Sunday of Easter** Acts 16:16–34 *Revelation 22:12–14,* *16–17, 20* John 17:20–26
The Holy Trinity Proverbs 8:1–4, 22–31 Romans 5:1–5 John 16:12–15	**The Holy Trinity** Proverbs 8:22–31 Romans 5:1–5 John 16:12–15	**The Holy Trinity** Isaiah 6:1–8 *Revelation 4:1–11* John 16:(5–11) 12–15

Revised Common	Roman Catholic	Episcopal
Proper 7	**12th Sunday in Ordinary Time**	**Proper 7**
1 Kings 19:1–15a	*Zechariah 12:10–11, 13:1*	*Zechariah 12:8–10, 13:1*
Galatians 3:23–29	Galatians 3:23–29	Galatians 3:23–29
Luke 8:26–39	Luke 9:18–24	Luke 9:18–24
Proper 26	**31st Sunday in Ordinary Time**	**Proper 26**
Habakkuk 1:1–4, 2:1–4	Wisdom 11:22–12:2	Isaiah 1:10–20
2 Thessalonians 1:1–4, 11–12	*2 Thessalonians 1:11–2:2*	*2 Thessalonians 1:1–5 (6–10) 11–12*
Luke 19:1–10	Luke 19:1–10	Luke 19:1–10
Proper 27	**32nd Sunday in Ordinary Time**	**Proper 27**
Haggai 1:15b–2:9	2 Maccabees 7:1–2, 9–14	Job 19:23–27a
2 Thessalonians 2:1–5, 13–17	*2 Thessalonians 2:16–3:5*	*2 Thessalonians 2:13–3:5*
Luke 20:27–38	Luke 20:27–38	Luke 20:27 (28–33) 34–38
Proper 28	**33rd Sunday in Ordinary Time**	**Proper 28**
Isaiah 65:17–25	Malachi 3:19–20	Malachi 3:13–4:2a, 5–6
2 Thessalonians 3:6–13	*2 Thessalonians 3:7–12*	*2 Thessalonians 3:6–14*
Luke 21:5–19	*Luke 21:5–19*	*Luke 21:5–19*
All Saints' Sunday	**All Saints' Sunday**	**All Saints' Sunday**
Daniel 7:1–3, 15–18	*Revelation 7:2–4, 9–14*	Ecclesiasticus (Sirach) 44:1–10, 13–14
Ephesians 1:11–23	1 John 3:1–3	*Revelation 7:2–4, 9–17*
Luke 6:20–31	Matthew 5:1–12	Matthew 5:1–12

NOTES

Book Epigraph

1. Oscar Romero, *The Violence of Love*, compiled and trans. by James R. Brockman, SJ (Farmington, PA: Plough Publishing, 1998), 25.

Introduction:
On the Path toward the Eternal Presence

1. Rainer Maria Rilke, *Letters to a Young Poet*, trans. Joan M. Burnham (Novato, CA: New World Library, 2000), 38.

2. The Roman Catholic Church uses the word homily for the preaching from the assigned lectionary readings by an ordained minister in the liturgical celebration. A homily is a short exposition of the readings meant to inspire the local congregation with the reading's applicability to today. In order to be ecumenically sensitive, the more general term, *sermon*, will be used throughout this work.

3. Jana Childers, *Performing the Word: Preaching as Theatre* (Nashville: Abingdon, 1998), 42.

4. David Buttrick, *Homiletic: Moves and Structures* (Philadelphia: Fortress, 1987), 482. Two noteworthy preaching books have appeared since Buttrick's comments were made: David Schnasa Jacobsen, *Preaching in the New Creation: The Promise of New Testament Apocalyptic Texts* (Louisville: Westminster John Knox Press, 1999) and Larry Paul Jones and Jerry L. Sumney, *Preaching Apocalyptic Texts* (St. Louis: Chalice Press, 1999).

5. George W. E. Nickelsburg, "The God of the Bible in a Nuclear Age?" *Currents in Theology and Mission* 11:4 (August 1984), 213.

6. Klaus Bäumlin, "Heaven and Earth Will Pass Away: Thoughts on Apocalyptic," *Theology Digest* 36:2 (1989), 141.

Chapter 1
Definition of Apocalyptic Literature

1. Widely circulated, especially online, as the "Romero Prayer," and attributed to Oscar Romero, the words were actually drafted by Bishop Ken Untener for a homily spoken by John Cardinal Dearden at a Mass for Romero. See www.nationalcatholicreporter.org/peace/pfg032804.htm

and, for the full prayer, http://bogners.typepad.com/church/2004/03/the_ prayer of_o.htm/. Subsequent references are to the "Romero Prayer."

2. John J. Collins, *The Apocalyptic Imagination: An Introduction to Jewish Apocalyptic Literature*, 2nd ed. (Grand Rapids, MI: Eerdmans Publishing Co., 1998), 1.

3. Catherine Keller, *Apocalypse Now and Then: A Feminist Guide to the End of the World* (Boston: Beacon Press, 1996) uses innovative readings of the Bible along with theology, philosophy, feminist theory, fiction and poetry, history, and current politics to show how the "myth of the apocalypse [speaking here specifically about the Book of Revelation] has shaped our basic habits of text, time, place, community, and gender."

4. Koester distinguishes between apocalypses and apocalyptic texts. He says that some of the elements of apocalypses "do appear in texts that are not, in themselves, apocalypses." These elements include the ordinary world being mysterious, revelation coming from a supernatural source, a hidden world of angels and demons, and a future judgment. Thus, the distinction is being made between apocalypses, which "bring these elements together in a narrative framework" and apocalyptic texts where only some of these elements appear. Craig R. Koester, *Revelation and the End of All Things* (Grand Rapids, MI: William B. Eerdmans Publishing Company, 2001), 28.

5. This definition is based on Paul D. Hanson, *Old Testament Apocalyptic: Interpreting Biblical Texts*, eds. Lloyd R. Bailey, Sr., and Victor P. Furnish (Nashville: Abingdon Press, 1987), 27–28, and on John J. Collins, *The Apocalyptic Imagination: An Introduction to Jewish Apocalyptic Literature*, 2nd ed. (Grand Rapids: Eerdmans Publishing Co., 1998), who quotes the Genres Project, a committee of the Society of Biblical Literature that investigated aspects of apocalyptic literature and published a definition in *Semeia* 14 (1979), 5.

Chapter 2
Walking toward Hope

1. Rainer Maria Rilke, *Letters to a Young Poet*, trans. Joan M. Burnham (Novato, CA: New World Library, 2000), 35.

2. Gary Braun, chaplain at Washington University, St. Louis, MO.

3. Jimmy Carter, interviewed by Terry Gross, *Fresh Air*, National Public Radio, December 5, 2001.

4. Thomas Aquinas, *Sum. Theol.*, IIa–IIae, q. 17, referenced in Clement Della Penta, OP, STLr, "Hope and Society: A Thomistic Study of Social Optimism and Pessimism, A Study in Social Philosophy" (PhD diss., Catholic University of America, vol. LXXXI, 1942), 13.

5. Ernst Bloch, *The Principle of Hope*, vol. 1, trans. Neville Plaice and others (Cambridge, MA: MIT Press, 1986), 3.

6. St. Thomas treats of supernatural hope, but does not give a complete definition in any one place. Aquinas, *Sum. Theol.* and *Questiones Disputatae de Spe, In III Sent.*, d. 26, q. 2, a. 1 are mentioned in Della Penta. This quote comes from page 13.

7. The most noble of all creatures is Jesus, the Christ, instrument of redemption for Christians. However, the saints in heaven and especially the Virgin Mary can aid Christians with hope.

8. It is true that Christians believe God has sent a messiah in Jesus the Christ, but they also believe that the Messiah will return. "People of the book" is characteristically used for the Jewish people, the Christian people, and the Muslim people, who all share belief in the first covenant of God with Abraham and all the nations forever. The emphasis here is on all people journeying down the same road toward the one God.

9. That same Son of man in the Second Testament represents Jesus, who was reviled, shamed, crushed, and subjected yet rises in glory to obliterate the enemies and leads the people to victory. Many Jewish people today accept their messianic role only in the sense that it relocates their people in a national home where violence from those who hate them ceases.

10. Jürgen Moltmann, *Theology of Hope: On the Ground and Implications of a Christian Eschatology*, trans. by James W. Leitch (New York: Harper & Row, 1967), 15.

11. Ibid., 26.

12. Augustine of Hippo, *The Confessions and Letters of St. Augustin, with a Sketch of His Life and Work*, vol. I, bk. 1. A Select Library of the Nicene and Post-Nicene Fathers of the Christian Church, ed. Philip Schaff (Grand Rapids, MI: Wm. B. Eerdmans Publishing Co., 1956), 45.

13. Michael Downey, *Hope Begins Where Hope Begins* (New York: Orbis Books, 1998), 14.

14. Glenn Tinder, *The Fabric of Hope: An Essay* (Atlanta: Scholars Press, 1999), 35–36.

15. Richard N. Fragomeni, *Come to the Feast: An Invitation to Eucharistic Transformation* (New York: Continuum, 1998), 29. This phrase is attributed to Irenaeus, a second-century church father.

16. See Jeremiah 29:10–11 for the best connection between promise and future. Some other passages that emphasize either promise or future are 1 Kings 8:56; 2 Kings 15:12; Jeremiah 31:17; Psalm 119:170; Proverbs 19:20, 23:18, and 24:14; Deuteronomy 9:5; 2 Samuel 7:21; Psalms 22:30 and 105:42.

17. Robert Ellsberg, *All Saints: Daily Reflections on Saints and Witnesses for Our Time*, November 7: Albert Camus (New York: Crossroad Publishing Co., 1997), 485.

18. Richard Rohr, "Days without Answers in a Narrow Space," *National Catholic Reporter* 38:13 (February 1, 2000), 14.

19. Ibid.

Chapter 3
Imagination and Apocalyptic Literature

1. Ted Loder, *Eavesdropping on the Echoes: Voices from the Old Testament* (San Diego: Lura Media, 1987), xiv.

2. Walter Brueggemann, *Finally Comes the Poet: Daring Speech for Proclamation* (Minneapolis: Fortress Press, 1989), 73.

3. The reign of Christ is the perspective of the Second Testament's Book of Revelation (see Rev 5:6–14). The First Testament proclaims the hope of a Son of man/messiah who will receive such praise (see Dan 7:13–14; Isa 26:1–12; and Ezek 14:6–20). See Daniel F. Hardy and David F. Ford, *Praising and Knowing God* (Philadelphia: Westminster Press, 1985), 11–13, for an opinion about praising God that is said to be dangerous, insidious, and subversive in today's world.

4. Loder, *Eavesdropping*, xiv.

5. Paul Scott Wilson, *Imagination of the Heart: New Understandings in Preaching* (Nashville: Abingdon, 1988).

6. Bishops' Committee on Priestly Life and Ministry, *Fulfilled in Your Hearing: The Homily in the Sunday Assembly* (Washington, DC: United States Catholic Conference, 1992), 25.

7. Wilson, *Imagination of the Heart*, 45.

8. Edward F. Markquart, *Quest for Better Preaching* (Minneapolis: Augsburg Press, 1985), 32.

9. See Exodus 3; Luke 1–2; and Ezekiel 37. Popular spirituals that arose from these texts include "Go Down, Moses," "Sweet Lil' Jesus Boy," and "Dem Bones Gonna Rise Again."

10. Thomas H. Troeger, *Preaching While the Church Is under Construction: The Visionary Role of Preacher in a Fragmented World* (Nashville: Abingdon, 1999), 21.

11. 9/11 has been used as an abbreviation for September 11, 2001.

12. Troeger, *Preaching*, 31.

Chapter 4
Tragic Theatre and Crisis

1. Loder, *Eavesdropping*, x.

2. Joan Delaplane, OP, Professor of Homiletics, Aquinas Institute of Theology, St. Louis, MO, after the mime prayer of the Gospel of Mark, November 1999.

3. The religious education director in a Catholic parish, Craig, Colorado, during Lent 1996, heard this comment from one attendee.

4. Andrew Carl Wisdom, OP, spoke these words after a performance for the Dominican Institute of Arts, July 2000.

5. A *mimesis* requires active reordering of poetic materials being utilized; it is like an imitation, but more fluid.

6. John Baxter and Patrick Atherton, eds., *Aristotle's Poetics*, trans. with commentary by George Whaley (Buffalo, NY: McGill-Queens University Press, 1997), 67 and 69.

7. Ibid., 69, 71, 73.

8. *American Heritage Dictionary of the English Language*, 4th ed. Available at: http://www.bartleby.com/61/55/D0115500.html.

9. Victor Turner, *From Ritual to Theatre: The Human Seriousness of Play* (New York: Performing Arts Journal Publications, 1982), 79.

10. Robert Cohen, *Acting Power* (Palo Alto, CA: Mayfield Publishing Co., 1978), 90.

11. Ibid., 33.

12. Ibid., 35.

13. Ibid., 108. Cohen also offers a series of exercises (109–10) for a person to practice this movement from past into future.

Chapter 5
Dramatic Crisis and Apocalyptic Literature

1. The "Romero Prayer."

2. Richard Schechner, *Ritual, Play and Performance* (New York: Seabury Press, 1977), 73–74, quoted in *From Ritual to Theatre: The Human Seriousness of Play* by Victor Turner (New York: Performing Arts Journal Publications, 1992). Figure 2, although not an exact replica, presents the same movements as the original.

3. Catherine Keller, *Apocalypse Now and Then: A Feminist Guide to the End of the World* (Boston: Beacon Press, 1996), 4.

4. Jana Childers, *Performing the Word: Preaching as Theatre* (Nashville: Abingdon, 1998), offers a chapter entitled "Worship as Theatre" (121–45). Stage-play changes to worship experience and audience changes to worshiping community.

5. Turner states that religion as art continues to live "insofar as it is being performed—in so far as its rituals are going concerns" (*From Ritual to Theatre*, 86).

6. Mark Olsen, *The Golden Buddha Changing Masks: Essays on the Spiritual Dimension of Acting* (Nevada City, CA: Gateways/IDHHB, 1989), 51.

7. Transference of energy comes from the science of physics. Interested readers may consult Ibid., 52–57, for a more detailed explanation of the science of energy.

8. Marva Dawn, Academy of Homiletics panel discussion, Dallas, December 1, 2000.

9. Childers, *Performing the Word*, 49.

10. Amos Wilder, "Electric Chimes and Ram's Horns," *Christian Century* 88 (January 27, 1971), 105.

11. Childers, *Performing the Word*, 39, citing M. James Young, lecture on "Church and Theatre," Wheaton, IL, 1975.

12. Olsen, *Golden Buddha*, 133–34.

13. Ibid., 134–42.

14. Martin Marty, *At the Edge of Hope*, Howard Butt and Elliot Wright, eds. (New York: Seabury Press, 1978), 175–77.

Chapter 6
Unmasking Apocalyptic Literature: Isaiah, Ezekiel

1. The "Romero Prayer."

2. Edward Hirsch, *How to Read a Poem and Fall in Love with Poetry*, A DoubleTakeBook published by the Center for Documentary Studies (New York: Harcourt Brace, 1999), 172–91, 173–74.

3. Ibid., 173.

4. Ibid., 174.

5. Helmer Ringgren, "Some Observations on Style and Structure in the Isaiah Apocalypse," *An Annual of the Swedish Theological Institute*, vol. 9 (Leiden: Brill, 1974), 107, quoted from J. Lindbloom, *Die Jesajaapokalypse*, *LU A* 1:34:3.

6. *NIV* Interlinear Version compares to the *REB*. The Jewish community commonly uses THE NAME for the unpronounceable YHWH, which has no vowels. Some Jewish people write G-d order to magnify its unpronounceable characteristic.

7. For those unfamiliar with the terms *focus* and *function*, see Thomas G. Long, *The Witness of Preaching* (Louisville: Westminister/John Knox Press, 1989), 86–91.

8. In the five short chapters identified as apocalyptic, the phrase "son of man" is used twelve times in the *NJB*: Ezekiel 2:1, 3, 6, 8; 3:1, 3, 4, 10; 38:2, 14; and 39:1, 17. This phrase is translated "mortal" in the *NRSV*.

9. Other translations use graphic words that fill in the feelings: "in a state of consternation" *(REB)*, "distraught" *(NABR)*, and "in a stupor" *(NJB)*.

10. Ralph W. Klein, Ezekiel: *The Prophet and His Message* (Columbia: University of South Carolina Press, 1988), 162. This was the only translation to use the graphic word *nose*.

Chapter 7
Unmasking Apocalyptic Literature:
Zechariah, Daniel

1. The "Romero Prayer."

2. Sister Marie Therese, Prioress of the Congregation of St. Catherine in Iraq, September 14, 2001, by e-mail from the Dominican Leadership Conference to the Grand Rapids Dominican Sisters, Grand Rapids, MI.

3. Paul L. Redditt, *The New Century Bible Commentary: Haggai, Zechariah, Malachi* from the series of New Century Bible Commentaries: Old Testament, ed. Ronald E. Clements (Grand Rapids: William B. Eerdmans Publishing Company, 1995), 109.

4. Paul D. Hanson, *The Dawn of Apocalyptic Eschatology: The Historical and Sociological Roots of Jewish Apocalyptic* (Philadelphia: Fortress Press, 1979), 316–19.

5. Other translations are "bowl of reeling" *(TNK)*, "intoxicating cup" *(REB)*, and "bowl to stupefy" *(NABR)*. See Jeremiah 25:15–17 or Habakkuk 2:16 for the image of God's wrath making nations shake or stagger. Amos 9:1 twists a little by having the shaking threshold be a manifestation of God's anger.

6. Refer to "Stirring Up the Great Sea: The Religio-Historical Background of Daniel 7," in *The Book of Daniel in the Light of New Findings*, ed. A. S. van der Woude (Leuven-Louvain, Belgium: Leuven University Press, 1993), 121–36.

7. Refer to John J. Collins, *The Apocalyptic Imagination: An Introduction to Jewish Apocalyptic Literature*, 2nd ed. (Grand Rapids, MI: Eerdmans Publishing Co., 1998), 101, for information about traditional motifs.

Chapter 8
Unmasking Apocalyptic Literature:
1 and 2 Thessalonians

1. Most scholars agree that Paul wrote seven letters: Romans, 1 and 2 Corinthians, Galatians, Philippians, 1 Thessalonians, and Philemon. Other letters, structured like Paul's authentic letters, may have been written by Paul but at a later period in his life. Early followers may have penned most other letters attributed to Paul.

2. For further insights on the Parousia, see Joseph Plevnik, *Paul and the Parousia: An Exegetical and Theological Investigation* (Peabody, MA: Hendrickson Publishers, 1997).

3. Colossians and Ephesians are the other two.

Chapter 9
Unmasking Apocalyptic Literature:
Synoptic Gospels

1. Patrick Marrin, "September 11, 2001," *National Catholic Reporter* (September 21, 2001), 11.

2. If your translation does not use "immediately," think the word *euthus* for a fast pace in this Gospel.

3. Readers can see these differences by using *Synopsis of the Four Gospels*, ed. Kurt Aland, from the Greek text of Nestle-Aland 26th ed. and Greek New Testament 3rd ed.; the biblical text is the 2nd ed. of the Revised Standard Version (United Bible Societies, 1965).

4. David Noel Freedman, ed., *Eerdmans Dictionary of the Bible* (Grand Rapids, MI: William B. Eerdmans Publishing Co., 2000), 236.

5. George T. Montague, SM, *Companion God: A Cross-Cultural Commentary of the Gospel of Matthew* (Mahwah, NJ: Paulist Press, 1989), 276. If readers wish to use a commentary to tackle the Gospel of Matthew, this commentary is very complete.

Chapter 10
Unmasking Apocalyptic Literature:
Book of Revelation

1. Yehuda Amicai, quoted by Daniel Berrigan, in *Isaiah: Spirit of Courage, Gift of Tears* (Minneapolis: Fortress Press, 1994), 42.

2. With some changes, this section was first published as an article by the author, "The Victory of the Lamb," *The Bible Today* (November 1993), 366–70.

3. There are many fine commentaries for studying the Book of Revelation. These are mentioned for the preacher/reader to begin their in-depth study. Craig R. Koester, *Revelation and the End of All Things* (Grand Rapids: Eerdmans Publishing Company, 2001). Pheme Perkins, "Revelation," in *The Collegeville Bible Commentary*, gen. eds. Dianne Bergant, CSA, and Robert J. Karris, OFM (Collegeville, MN: Liturgical Press, 1989), 1265–1300. This commentary is also available in a single-copy edition from your local bookstore; Seán P. Kealy, CSSp, *The Apocalypse of John* (Wilmington, DE: Michael Glazier, 1987); Adela Yarbro Collins, *The Apocalypse*, New Testament Message 22 (Wilmington, DE: Michael Glazier, 1985); Elisabeth Schüssler Fiorenza, Revelation: Vision of a Just World, Proclamation Commentaries, Gerhard Krodel, ed. (Minneapolis: Fortress Press, 1991). There is also a guided discovery by Kevin Perrotta, *Revelation: God's Gift of Hope* (Chicago: Loyola Press, 2000).

Chapter 11
Moving toward Christian Action with Hope

1. Marcel Proust (1871–1922), quoted in Joseph Cornell, *With Beauty before Me*, © 2000. Available at: http://www.sharingnature.com/beauty/beautynew2.html.

2. "Faith community" is used instead of "church" in order to embrace all faiths.

3. Cardinal Paulo Evaristo Arns, "From Hope to Hope," *National Catholic Reporter* (April 4, 2003), 11.

4. Jürgen Moltmann, *Theology of Hope: On the Ground and Implications of a Christian Eschatology*, trans. by James W. Leitch (New York: Harper & Row, 1967), 122–23.

5. See *Dogmatic Constitution on the Church*, in Walter M. Abbott, SJ, gen. ed., *The Documents of Vatican II* (New York: America Press, 1966), 31.

6. Oscar Romero, *The Violence of Love*, compiled and trans. by James R. Brockman, SJ (Farmington, PA: Plough Publishing, 1998), 1.

7. Jürgen Moltmann, "Love, Death, Eternal Life: Theology of Hope—The Personal Side," in Frederic B. Burnham, Charles S. McCoy, and M. Douglas Meeks, eds., *Love: The Foundation of Hope—The Theology of Jürgen Moltmann and Elisabeth Moltmann-Wendel* (San Francisco: Harper & Row, 1988), 5.

8. M. Douglas Meeks, "Love and Hope for a Just Society," in Burnham et al. *Love*, 50.

9. José Míguez Bonino, "Love and Social Transformation in Liberation Theology," in Burnham et al., *Love*, 80–89.

10. James H. Cone, *Black Theology and Black Power* (New York: Seabury Press, 1969), 43, quoted in *Black Awareness: A Theology of Hope* by Major J. Jones (Nashville: Abingdon, 1971), 15.

11. An excellent theological exegesis recently published will further assist the preacher in these days of crisis as well as hope. Roger E. Van Harn, ed., *The Lectionary Commentary: Theological Exegesis for Sunday's Texts*, 3 vols. (Grand Rapids, MI: William B. Eerdmans Publishing Co., 2001).

12. Walter Brueggemann, *Finally Comes the Poet: Daring Speech for Proclamation* (Minneapolis: Fortress Press, 1989), 59.

13. Joseph R. Jeter Jr., *Crisis Preaching: Personal and Public* (Nashville: Abingdon, 1998), 81.

14. Howard Butt with Elliott Wright, *At the Edge of Hope: Christian Laity in Paradox* (New York: Seabury Press, 1978), 180.

15. *Democrat and Chronicle* (Rochester, NY), December 2, 2001.

16. Jürgen Moltmann, *Theology of Play*, trans. by Reinhard Ulrich (New York: Harper & Row, Publishers, 1972), 57–58.

17. Micah 6:8. Other books that might be helpful for connecting hope to justice are Walter Wink, *The Powers That Be: Theology for a New*

Millennium (New York: A Galilee Book Published by Doubleday, 1998); Daniel Berrigan, *Daniel: Under the Siege of the Divine* (Farmington, PA: Plough Publishing, 1998); Kevin O'Shea, *Person in Cosmos: Metaphors of Meaning from Physics, Philosophy and Theology* (Bristol, IN: Wyndham Hall Press, 1995); John A. Sanford, *Evil: The Shadow Side of Reality* (New York: Crossroad Publishing Co., 2001); Kerry Walters, *Godlust: Facing the Demonic, Embracing the Divine* (New York: Paulist Press, 1999); René Girard, *I See Satan Falling Like Lightning*, trans. by James G. Williams (Maryknoll, NY: Orbis Books, 2001); and André Biéler, *The Politics of Hope*, trans. by Dennis Pardee (Grand Rapids, MI: William B. Eerdmans Publishing Co., 1974).

18. Figure 3 was found in Fritz West, *Scripture and Memory: The Ecumenical Hermeneutic of the Three-Year Lectionaries* (Collegeville, MN: Liturgical Press, 1997), 73.

19. Ibid., 82–83, for this diagram of overlapping circles that shows the entire configuration.

20. *Revised Common Lectionary* (Nashville: Abingdon, 1992), 14.

21. West, *Scripture and Memory*, 74.

22. Ibid., 76–87, offers a number of specific examples that might be helpful for further reflection. For additional reflection on apocalyptic literature, see my article, "Victory of the Lamb: A Look at the Book of Revelation," *The Bible Today* (November 1993). For additional reflection on hope, see Gregory Baum, "The Meaning of Hope in Evil Times," *L'ARC* (Spring 1992), 79–83.

Chapter 12
A Plan for My Life:
Preaching and Teaching

1. Demetrius Dumm, "Why Apocalyptic Gospels in Advent," *Worship* 63 (November 1989), 483.

2. Jeff Daniel, "Looking behind the Masks," *St. Louis Post-Dispatch* (October 10, 1999), F-1.

3. Karl Rahner, "Nature and Grace," in *Nature and Grace* (New York: Sheed & Ward, 1963), 134; quoted in Mary Catherine Hilkert, *Naming Grace: Preaching and the Sacramental Imagination* (New York: Continuum, 1998), 33.

4. Craig R. Dykstra, *Vision and Character: A Christian Educator's Alternative to Kohlberg* (New York: Paulist Press, 1981), 51; quoted in Richard L. Eslinger, *Narrative Imagination: Preaching the Worlds That Shape Us* (Minneapolis: Fortress Press, 1995), 89.

5. Eslinger, *Narrative Imagination*, 27.

6. Buttrick, *Homiletic*, 457.

7. John Koize, news release for *Revisit Bible Stories to Understand Your Life Story* by Macrina Scott, OSF (Cincinnati, OH: St. Anthony Messenger Press), received November 1999.

8. Joseph M. Webb, *Preaching and the Challenge of Pluralism* (St. Louis: Chalice Press, 1998), 59–60.

9. Buttrick, *Homiletic*, 457. He says later, "Good Heavens, what a vocation!" when asked to represent that Presence-in-Absence to the community of faith.

10. Walter Wink's book *Engaging the Powers: Discernment and Resistance in a World of Domination* (Minneapolis: Fortress Press, 1992) is the third in a trilogy of books about systems of power in the Bible.

11. James H. Cone, *Speaking the Truth: Ecumenism, Liberation, and Black Theology* (Maryknoll, NY: Orbis Books, 1986), 58.

12. Preached for the community of St. Jerome, Troy, IL, in November 2000, by Dorothy Jonaitis, OP.

13. Homily given by Gregory Heille, OP, at a school Eucharist for those who have died and are suffering, September 13, 2001, Aquinas Institute of Theology, St. Louis, MO.

14. The U.S. decision to go to war in both Afghanistan and Iraq shortly after the 9/11 crisis shows that the United States government, supported by quite a few of its citizens, is not able to speak a truth in nonviolent words and actions. It behooves us to carry the truth of nonviolence in our lives and to speak out whenever we can that violence will just beget more violence. This truth, that violence will cause more violence, is playing itself out each day as our withdrawal from Iraq is delayed because suicide bombers are killing more and more innocent victims.

Chapter 13
Theology of Preaching/Teaching

1. Interested readers may find other preaching theologies in *Theology of Preaching: Essays on Vision and Mission in the Pulpit*, ed. Gregory Heille, OP (London: Melisende, 2001).

2. You can visit www.oprah.com for more information, or you can write to Oprah's Angel Network, P.O. Box 96600, Chicago, IL 60693.

3. Oprah Winfrey, "Christmas Kindness," *The Oprah Winfrey Show*, December 22, 2003.

4. Ibid.

5. Elizabeth A. Johnson, *She Who Is: The Mystery of God in Feminist Theological Discourse* (New York: Crossroad, 1993), 33.

6. Robert A. Ludwig, *Reconstructing Catholicism for a New Generation* (New York: Crossroad, 1996), 98.

7. Roberto S. Goizueta, *Caminemos con Jesus: Toward a Hispanic/Latino Theology of Accompaniment* (Maryknoll, NY: Orbis Books, 1995), 34.

8. E. E. Cummings, no title, n.d.; quoted in Ludwig, *Reconstructing Catholicism*, 146.

9. Judith Fetterly, "The Resisting Reader: A Feminist Approach to American Fiction" in *Mark and Method: New Approaches in Biblical Studies*, eds. Janice Capel Anderson and Stephen D. Moore (Minneapolis: Fortress Press, 1992), 73.

10. The movie *Dogma* unmasks funny religious clichés. The hermeneutics of violence was not appreciated.

11. Cone, *Speaking the Truth*, 113.

Appendix:
Apocalyptic Texts on Sundays and Major Feasts

1. The guide for making this chart of apocalyptic readings was Russell Anderson, *Lectionary Preaching Workbook*, Series V, Cycles A, B, C (Lima, OH: CSS Publishing Company, 1995).

BIBLIOGRAPHY

Adler, William. "The Apocalyptic Survey of History Adapted by Christians: Daniel's Prophecy of 70 Weeks." In *The Jewish Apocalyptic Heritage in Early Christianity*. Assen, Netherlands: Van Gorcum, 1998, 201–22.

Aland, Kurt, ed. *Synopsis of the Four Gospels*, from the Greek text of Nestle-Aland 26th ed. and Greek New Testament 3rd ed.; the biblical text is the 2nd ed. of the Revised Standard Version. United Bible Societies, 1965.

American Heritage Dictionary of the English Language, 4th ed. Available at http://www.bartleby.com/61/55/D0115500.html.

Anderson, Janice Capel and Stephen D. Moore, eds. *Mark and Method: New Approaches in Biblical Studies*. Minneapolis: Fortress Press, 1992.

Anderson, Russell. *Lectionary Preaching Workbook*, Series V, Cycles A, B, C. Lima, OH: CSS Publishing Company, 1997.

Aquinas, Thomas. *Questiones Disputatae de Spe. In III Sent.*, d. 26, q. 2, a.1 Quoted in Clement Della Penta, OP. "Hope and Society: A Thomistic Study of Social Optimism and Pessimism, A Study in Social Philosophy." PhD diss., Catholic University of America, 1942.

———. *Summa Theologiae*, IIa–IIae, q. 17. Blackfriars, in conjunction with New York: McGraw-Hill Book Co., 1964.

Arns, Cardinal Paulo Evaristo. "From Hope to Hope." *National Catholic Reporter* (April 4, 2003).

Augustine of Hippo. *The Confessions and Letters of St. Augustin, with a Sketch of His Life and Work*, vol. 1, bk. 1. A Select Library of the Nicene and Post-Nicene Fathers of the Christian Church, ed. Philip Schaff. (Grand Rapids, MI: Wm. B. Eerdmans Publishing Co., 1956).

Bauerschmidt, Frederick. "Can Mystics Matter?" *National Catholic Reporter* 38: 13 (February 1, 2002).

Baum, Gregory. "The Meaning of Hope in Evil Times." *L'ARC* (Spring 1992).

Bäumlin, Klaus. "Heaven and Earth Will Pass Away: Thoughts on Apocalyptic." *Theology Digest* 36: 2 (1989).

Baxter, John and Patrick Atherton, eds. *Aristotle's Poetics*. Trans. with commentary by George Whaley. Buffalo, NY: McGill-Queens University Press, 1997.

Bartlett, David L. *Between the Bible and the Church: New Methods for Biblical Preaching*. Nashville: Abingdon, 1999.

Berquist, Jon L. *Judaism in Persia's Shadow: A Social and Historical Approach*. Minneapolis: Fortress Press, 1995.

Berrigan, Daniel. *Daniel: Under the Siege of the Divine*. Farmington, PA: Plough Publishing, 1998.

———. *Isaiah: Spirit of Courage, Gift of Tears*. Minneapolis: Fortress Press, 1994.

Biddle, Mark E. "The City of Chaos and the New Jerusalem: Isaiah 24–27 in Context." *Perspectives-in-Religious-Studies* 22 (Spring 1995): 5–12.

Biéler, André. *The Politics of Hope.* Trans. by Dennis Pardee. Grand Rapids, MI.: William B. Eerdmans Publishing Co., 1974.

Bishops' Committee on Priestly Life and Ministry. *Fulfilled in Your Hearing: The Homily in the Sunday Assembly.* Washington DC: United States Catholic Conference, 1992.

Bloch, Ernst. *The Principle of Hope,* vol. 1. Trans. Neville Plaice and others. Cambridge, MA: MIT Press, 1986.

Bonino, José Míguez. "Love and Social Transformation in Liberation Theology." In *Love: The Foundation of Hope—The Theology of Jürgen Moltmann and Elisabeth Moltmann-Wendel,* edited by Frederic B. Burnham and others. San Francisco: Harper & Row, 1988.

Brueggemann, Walter. *Finally Comes the Poet: Daring Speech for Proclamation.* Minneapolis: Fortress Press, 1989.

———. *Texts under Negotiation: The Bible and Postmodern Imagination.* Minneapolis: Fortress Press, 1993.

———. *The Threat of Life: Sermons on Pain, Power, and Weakness.* Edited by Charles L. Campbell. Minneapolis: Fortress Press, 1996.

Burnham, Frederic B., Charles S. McCoy, and M. Douglas Meeks, eds. *Love: The Foundation of Hope—The Theology of Jürgen Moltmann and Elisabeth Moltmann-Wendel.* San Francisco: Harper & Row, 1988.

Butt, Howard with Elliott Wright. *At the Edge of Hope: Christian Laity in Paradox.* New York: Seabury Press, 1978.

Buttrick, David. *Homiletic: Moves and Structures.* Philadelphia: Fortress, 1987.

Carey, Gary and L. Gregory Bloomquist. *Vision and Persuasion: Rhetorical Dimensions of Apocalyptic Discourse.* St. Louis: Chalice Press, 1999.

Carter, Jimmy. Interview by Terry Gross, *Fresh Air.* National Public Radio, December 5, 2001.

Childers, Jana. *Performing the Word: Preaching as Theatre.* Nashville: Abingdon, 1998.

Coggins, R. J. *Haggai, Zechariah, Malachi.* Old Testament Guides, R. N. Whybray, ed. Sheffield, UK: Sheffield Academy Press, 1996.

Cohen, Robert. *Acting Power.* Palo Alto, CA: Mayfield Publishing Co., 1978.

Collins, Adela Yarbro. *The Apocalypse.* New Testament Message 22. Wilmington, DE: Michael Glazier, 1985.

Collins, John J. *The Apocalyptic Imagination: An Introduction to Jewish Apocalyptic Literature,* 2nd ed. The Biblical Resource Series. Grand Rapids, MI: William B. Eerdmans Publishing Co., 1998.

———. *Daniel: A Commentary on the Book of Daniel.* Minneapolis: Fortress Press, 1993.

The Complete Parallel Bible Containing the Old and New Testaments with the Apocryphal and Deuterocanonical Books, 1st ed. New York: Oxford University Press, 1993.

Cone, James H. *Black Theology and Black Power.* New York: Seabury Press, 1969.

———. *Speaking the Truth: Ecumenism, Liberation, and Black Theology.* Maryknoll, NY: Orbis Books, 1986.

Conrad, Edgar W. *Zechariah.* Sheffield, UK: Sheffield Academic Press, 1999.

Daniel, Jeff. "Looking behind the Masks." *St. Louis Post-Dispatch,* October 10, 1999.

Dearden, John Cardinal, popularly attributed to Romero, Oscar. *Prophets of a Future Not Our Own, A Prayer by Archbishop Oscar Romero.* Available at: http://rrnet.com/~sedaqah/oarpry.htm.

Della Penta, Clement OP, STLr. "Hope and Society: A Thomistic Study of Social Optimism and Pessimism, A Study in Social Philosophy." PhD. diss, Catholic University of America, 1942.

Dogmatic Constitution on the Church, in Walter M. Abbott, SJ, gen. ed., *The Documents of Vatican II.* New York: America Press, 1966.

Downey, Michael. *Hope Begins Where Hope Begins.* New York: Orbis Books, 1998.

Dumm, Demetrius. "Why Apocalyptic Gospels in Advent?" *Worship* 63 (November 1989): 482–89.

Dykstra, Craig R. *Vision and Character: A Christian Educator's Alternative to Kohlberg.* New York: Paulist Press, 1981.

Ellsberg, Robert. *All Saints: Daily Reflections on Saints and Witnesses for Our Time.* November 7: Albert Camus. New York: Crossroad Publishing Co., 1997.

Erskine, Noel L. "Christian Hope and the Black Experience." In *Hope for the Church: Moltman in Dialogue with Practical Theology*, Jürgen Moltman with M. Douglas Meeks. Ed. and trans. by Theodore Runyan. Nashville: Abingdon, 1979.

Eslinger, Richard L. *Narrative Imagination: Preaching the Worlds That Shape Us.* Minneapolis: Fortress Press, 1995.

Feinberg, Charles. *God Remembers: A Study of Zechariah*, 4th ed. Portland, OR: Multnomah Press, 1979.

Fetterly, Judith. "The Resisting Reader: A Feminist Approach to American Fiction." In *Mark and Method: New Approaches in Biblical Studies*, edited by Janice Capel Anderson and Stephen D. Moore. Minneapolis: Fortress Press, 1992.

Fiorenza, Elisabeth Schüssler. *Revelation: Vision of a Just World.* Proclamation Commentaries, Gerhard Krodel, ed. Minneapolis: Fortress Press, 1991.

Fragomeni, Richard N. *Come to the Feast: An Invitation to Eucharistic Transformation.* New York: Continuum, 1998.

Freedman, David Noel, ed. *Eerdmans Dictionary of the Bible.* Grand Rapids, MI: William B. Eerdmans Publishing Co., 2000.

Girard, René. *I See Satan Falling Like Lightning.* Trans. by James G. Williams. Maryknoll, NY: Orbis Books, 2001.

"Giving Voice to Hope." *Living with Christ* (November 2001).

Goizueta, Roberto S. *Caminemos con Jesus: Toward a Hispanic/Latino Theology of Accompaniment.* Maryknoll, NY: Orbis Books, 1995.

Hanson, Paul D. *Apocalypses and Apocalypticism.* Oak Harbor, WA: Logos Library System, 1998.

————. *The Dawn of Apocalyptic Eschatology: The Historical and Sociological Roots of Jewish Apocalyptic.* Philadelphia: Fortress Press, 1979.

————. *Old Testament Apocalyptic: Interpreting Biblical Texts.* Edited by Lloyd R. Bailey Sr. and Victor P. Furnish. Nashville: Abingdon, 1987.

Hardy, Daniel F. and David F. Ford. *Praising and Knowing God.* Philadelphia: Westminster Press, 1985.

Heille, Gregory, OP, ed. *Theology of Preaching: Essays on Vision and Mission in the Pulpit.* London: Melisende, 2001.

Herzog, Frederick, ed. *The Future of Hope: Theology as Eschatology*. New York: Herder & Herder, 1970.

Hilkert, Mary Catherine. *Naming Grace: Preaching and the Sacramental Imagination*. New York: Continuum, 1998.

Hirsch, Edward. *How to Read a Poem and Fall in Love with Poetry*. New York: Harcourt Brace, 1999.

Jacobsen, David Schnasa. *Preaching in the New Creation: The Promise of New Testament Apocalyptic Texts*. Louisville: Westminster John Knox Press, 1999.

Jeter, Joseph R. Jr. *Crisis Preaching: Personal and Public*. Nashville: Abingdon, 1998.

Johnson, Elizabeth A. *She Who Is: The Mystery of God in Feminist Theological Discourse*. New York: Crossroad, 1993.

Jonaitis, Dorothy, OP. "The Victory of the Lamb." *The Bible Today* (November 1993).

Jones, Larry Paul and Jerry L. Sumney. *Preaching Apocalyptic Texts*. St. Louis: Chalice Press, 1999.

Jones, Major J. *Black Awareness: A Theology of Hope*. Nashville: Abingdon, 1971.

Kealy, Seán P., CSSp. *The Apocalypse of John*. Wilmington, DE: Michael Glazier, 1987.

Keller, Catherine. *Apocalypse Now and Then: A Feminist Guide to the End of the World*. Boston: Beacon Press, 1996.

Klein, Ralph W. *Ezekiel: The Prophet and His Message*. Columbia: University of South Carolina Press, 1988.

Koester, Craig R. *Revelation and the End of All Things*. Grand Rapids: Eerdmans Publishing Company, 2001.

Koize, John. News release for *Revisit Bible Stories to Understand Your Life Story* by Macrina Scott, OSF. Cincinnati, OH: St. Anthony Messenger Press, November 1999.

Law, Eric R. *The Wolf Shall Dwell with the Lamb: A Spirituality for Leadership in a Multicultural Community*. St. Louis: Chalice Press, 1993.

Loder, Ted. *Eavesdropping on the Echoes: Voices from the Old Testament*. San Diego: Lura Media, 1987.

Long, Thomas G. *The Witness of Preaching*. Louisville: Westminster/John Knox Press, 1989.

Ludwig, Robert A. *Reconstructing Catholicism for a New Generation*. New York: Crossroad, 1996.

Malina, Bruce J. *The New Jerusalem in the Revelation of John: The City as Symbol of Life with God*. Collegeville, MN: Liturgical Press, 1995.

Markquart, Edward F. *Quest for Better Preaching*. Minneapolis: Augsburg Press, 1985.

Marrin, Patrick. "September 11, 2001." *National Catholic Reporter* (September 21, 2001).

Marty, Martin. *At the Edge of Hope*. Edited by Howard Butt and Elliot Wright. New York: Seabury Press, 1978.

Meyers, Carol L. and Eric M. Meyers. *Zechariah 9–14: A New Translation with Introduction and Commentary*, 1st ed. Anchor Bible Series. New York: Doubleday, 1993.

Meeks, M. Douglas. "Love and Hope for a Just Society." In *Love: The Foundation of Hope—The Theology of Jürgen Moltmann and Elisabeth Moltmann-Wendel*, edited by Frederic B. Burnham and others. San Francisco: Harper & Row, 1988.

Metzger, Bruce M. and Roland E. Murphy, eds. *The New Oxford Annotated Bible with the Apocryphal/Deuterocanonical Books.* New York: Oxford University Press, 1994.

Mitchell, Henry H. *Black Preaching: The Recovery of a Powerful Art.* Nashville: Abingdon, 1990.

Moltmann, Jürgen. "Love, Death, Eternal Life: Theology of Hope—The Personal Side." In *Love: The Foundation of Hope—The Theology of Jürgen Moltmann and Elisabeth Moltmann-Wendel,* edited by Frederic B. Burnham and others. San Francisco: Harper & Row, 1988.

———. *Theology of Hope: On the Ground and Implications of a Christian Eschatology.* Trans. by James W. Leitch. New York: Harper & Row, 1967.

———. *Theology of Play.* Trans. by Reinhard Ulrich. New York: Harper & Row, 1972.

Montague, George T., SM. *Companion God: A Cross-Cultural Commentary of the Gospel of Matthew.* Mahwah, NJ: Paulist Press, 1989.

Moyd, Olin P. *The Sacred Art: Preaching and Theology in the African American Tradition.* Valley Forge, PA: Judson Press, 1995.

Nicklesburg, George W. E. "The God of the Bible in a Nuclear Age?" *Currents in Theology and Mission* 11:4 (August 1984).

Olsen, Mark. *The Golden Buddha Changing Masks: Essays on the Spiritual Dimension of Acting.* Nevada City, CA: Gateways/IDHHB, 1989.

O'Shea, Kevin. *Person in Cosmos: Metaphors of Meaning from Physics, Philosophy and Theology.* Bristol, IN: Wyndham Hall Press, 1995.

Pagan, Samuel. "Apocalyptic Poetry: Isaiah 24–27." *The Bible Translator* 43:3 (1992): 314–25.

Perkins, Pheme. "Revelation." In *The Collegeville Bible Commentary,* gen. eds. Dianne Bergant, CSA, and Robert J. Karris, OFM. Collegeville, MN: Liturgical Press, 1989, 1265–1300.

Perrotta, Kevin. *Revelation: God's Gift of Hope.* Chicago: Loyola Press, 2000.

Plevnik, Joseph. *Paul and the Parousia: An Exegetical and Theological Investigation.* Peabody, MA: Hendrickson Publishers, 1997.

Rahner, Karl. "Nature and Grace." In *Nature and Grace.* New York: Sheed & Ward, 1963.

Redditt, Paul L. *The New Century Bible Commentary: Haggai, Zechariah, Malachi.* Publication in Series of New Century Bible Commentaries: Old Testament. Ed., Ronald E. Clements. Grand Rapids: William B. Eerdmans Publishing Company, 1995.

Revised Common Lectionary. Nashville: Abingdon, 1992.

Rice, Charles L. *Interpretation and Imagination: The Preacher and Contemporary Literature.* Philadelphia: Fortress Press, 1970.

Rilke, Rainer Maria. *Letters to a Young Poet.* Trans. by Joan M. Burnham. Novato, CA: New World Library, 2000.

Ringgren, Helmer. "Some Observations on Style and Structure in the Isaiah Apocalypse." *An Annual of the Swedish Theological Institute,* vol. 9. Leiden: Brill, 1974.

Rohr, Richard. "Days without Answers in a Narrow Space." *National Catholic Reporter* 38:13 (February 1, 2000).

Romero, Oscar. *The Violence of Love*. Compiled and trans. by James R. Brockman, SJ. Farmington, PA: Plough Publishing, 1998.

Russell, D. S. *Prophecy and the Apocalyptic Dream: Protest and Promise*. Peabody, MA: Henrickson Publishers, 1994.

Sanford, John A. *Evil: The Shadow Side of Reality*. New York: Crossroad Publishing Co., 2001.

Schechner, Richard. *Ritual, Play and Performance*. New York: Seabury Press, 1977.

Smith, Christine M. *Preaching as Weeping, Confession, and Resistance: Radical Responses to Evil*. Louisville: Westminster John Knox Press, 1992.

Tanakh, The Holy Scriptures: The New JPS Translation According to the Traditional Hebrew Text. Philadelphia: Jewish Publication Society, 1985.

Taylor, Barbara Brown. *God in Pain: Teaching Sermons on Suffering*. The Teaching Sermon Series, ed. Ronald J. Allen. Nashville: Abingdon, 1998.

————. *Speaking of Sin: The Lost Language of Salvation*. Boston: Cowley Publications, 2000.

Tinder, Glenn. *The Fabric of Hope: An Essay*. Atlanta: Scholars Press, 1999.

Troeger, Thomas H. *Preaching While the Church Is under Construction: The Visionary Role of Preacher in a Fragmented World*. Nashville: Abingdon, 1999.

Turner, Victor. *From Ritual to Theatre: The Human Seriousness of Play*. New York: Performing Arts Journal Publications, 1992.

Tutu, Desmond. *Hope and Suffering: Sermons and Speeches*. Compiled by Mothobi Mutloatse, edited by John Webster. Grand Rapids, MI: William B. Eerdmans Publishing, 1984.

Van der Woude, A. S., ed. "Stirring Up the Great Sea: The Religio-Historical Background of Daniel 7." In *The Book of Daniel in the Light of New Findings*. Leuven-Louvain, Belgium: Leuven University Press, 1993.

Van Harn, Roger E., ed. *The Lectionary Commentary: Theological Exegesis for Sunday's Texts*, 3 vols. (Grand Rapids, MI: William B. Eerdmans Publishing Co., 2001).

Walters, Kerry. *Godlust: Facing the Demonic, Embracing the Divine*. New York: Paulist Press, 1999.

Webb, Joseph M. *Preaching and the Challenge of Pluralism*. St. Louis: Chalice Press, 1998.

West, Fritz. *Scripture and Memory: The Ecumenical Hermeneutic of the Three-Year Lectionaries*. Collegeville, MN: Liturgical Press, 1997.

Wilder, Amos. "Electric Chimes and Ram's Horns." *Christian Century* 88 (January 27, 1971): 105.

Wilson, Paul Scott. *Imagination of the Heart: New Understandings in Preaching*. Nashville: Abingdon, 1988.

Wink, Walter. *Engaging the Powers: Discernment and Resistance in a World of Domination*. Minneapolis: Fortress Press, 1992.

————. *The Powers That Be: Theology for a New Millennium*. New York: A Galilee Book Published by Doubleday, 1998.

Witherup, Ronald D., SS. "Apocalyptic Imagery in the Book of Ezekiel." *The Bible Today* 37:1 (January/February 1999): 10–17.